STRIKE

STRIKE

U.S. Naval Strike Warfare Center

Text by John Joss
Photography by George Hall

Presidio Press ★ Novato, California
THE PRESIDIO POWER SERIES
AIRPOWER #1008

Published by Presidio Press
31 Pamaron Way, Novato CA 94949

LIBRARY OF CONGRESS
Library of Congress Cataloging-in-Publication Data

Joss, John, 1934–
    Strike: U.S. Naval Strike Warfare Center/text by John Joss;
photography by George Hall.
        p.   cm.   (The Presidio power series. Airpower; #1008)
    ISBN 0–89141–320–0:
    1. Naval Strike Warfare Center (Nev.)   2. Bombing, Aerial—Study
and teaching—United States.   3. Attack planes—United States.
I. Hall, George (George N.)   II. Title.—III. Series.
VG94.5.N63J67 1988
358.4′3—dc 19   88–10186
                                                       CIP

Photographs Copyright © by George Hall, with the following exceptions:
John Joss, 20–21, 117

Printed in the United States of America
Title page: Strike faculty TA-7 unleashes a 5-inch Zuni rocket over the Bravo-17 range.

Contents

Acknowledgments

The enormous popularity attained, deservedly, by the *Top Gun* film, book, and video tended to overshadow one of the other vital elements of naval aviation—the attack community. The attack community is sometimes perceived as a little less glamorous, exciting, and interesting. Don't believe this? Ask any fighter community pilot . . . In fact, the attack community is the fundamental reason for the existence of naval aviation within the United States Navy. In practice, the fighter community is a part of the overall mission and effort.

For these and for many other reasons, we were greeted with enthusiasm and kindness by the entire Strike staff. These pros wanted to see their story told. Their only restraints, based on security, were in details of scenarios trained, since these are core Navy operational tactics. In all other respects, nothing was too much trouble for this great group of men and women.

At Strike we were briefed in depth by the skipper, Capt. Robert G. ("Bubba") Brodsky, and by his XO, Comdr. Bob Knowles. Technical Director Dr. Roger Whiteway (himself an A-6 driver and key in Strike's formation) provided essential background detail. All the specialists in the various areas briefed us to the extent permitted by security restrictions. These included, in particular, Comdr. Jon Green, intelligence department head, and Lt. Jeff Stratton of the SEALS. Range Officer Comdr. "Sandy" Sanford of the NAS Fallon staff helped greatly in discussing the range setup vital to Strike's overall curriculum. Special thanks also to Comdr. John ("Wurm") Henson, who was changing jobs, leaving to become skipper of VA-55, an East Coast A-6 squadron. He coordinated our schedules and took valuable time when he must have had more important things to do.

We couldn't have attempted this project without flying in current attack community aircraft. Both of us were treated to body-bending experiences in the TA-7 Corsair II with Lt. Comdr. Craig ("Slim") Henderson. In the F/A-18 Hornet, John Joss flew an ACM hop with the XO of Cecil Field's Hornet RAG, VFA-106, Lt. Col. Vic ("Clam") Simpson. George Hall flew with Lt. ("Steely") Dan Dealey and Mike "Trapper" Spence for additional fam and photos. Steely and his colleagues went over the manuscript carefully and were brutally candid and helpful in their suggested revisions.

This is not the complete story of Strike. It is really told daily in the challenging training and operational work of the U.S. Navy carrier air wings and in the results they achieve, often in the face of great adversity. We salute them.

John Joss
George Hall

Previous pages: A-7 and A-6 attack birds demonstrate terrain masking prior to rocket attack.

Right: Strike instructor and iron weaponry expert "Steely" Dan Dealey.

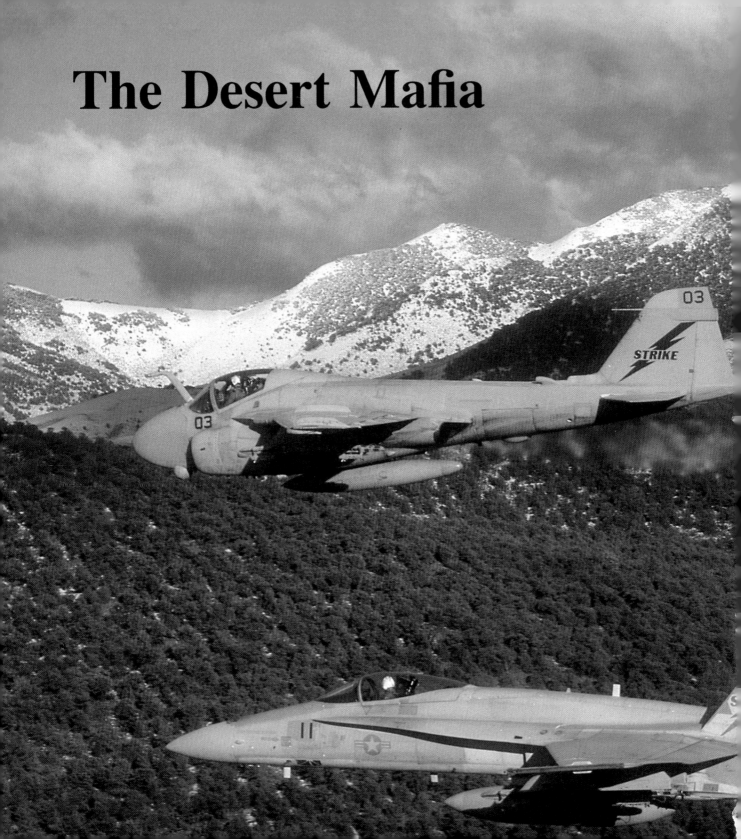

The Desert Mafia

"mafia: n. a secret society"
—Webster

In summer, Fallon, Nevada, roasts in the desert high country of the western United States. In winter, and many spring and fall nights, it freezes. Hotter than the hubs of hell or colder than charity. Take your pick. It has been this way for at least four thousand years, since Nevada's inland lakes evaporated and the benign climate they fostered changed to savage extremes. Either way, today, not everyone considers it the garden spot of the Western world.

To easterners or Europeans, or those used to at least a modicum of green, a sympathetic environment, the whitish alkali lake beds and barren brown and grey mountains of modern Nevada are almost a physical assault on the spirit. Sensitive souls tend to curl at the edges, dry up, blow away. The desert does not care. It never has; it never will. If you find the surface of the moon congenial, it ain't bad.

When the airfield at Fallon was established in the 1940s, it was out of the aviation mainstream, just an Army auxiliary airfield used to train Army Air Corps pilots. NAS Fallon was formally commissioned as a naval air station as recently as 1972.

Today, naval aviators *want* to go there, primarily because of Strike. The new boonies for the

misbegotten? Diego Garcia or Adak. Fallon, sixty miles east of Reno, is a town of 5,000 that, except for NAS Fallon and Strike, is graced only by gambling, guns, and agriculture. That's all there is, or really ever was. So why in the world would the Navy want to buy into the area?

The Navy wanted it for the same reason the Air Corps (and later the Air Force) wanted to be in Nevada—300+ days per year CAVU (ceiling and visibility unlimited) flying (admittedly, the remaining days deliver snow, ice, severe turbulence, and blowing sand). But compared with Nellis, about 400 miles to the south, just north of Las Vegas and athwart the major airways from the East and Middle West to Los Angeles and San Diego, Fallon offers the advantage of minimal commercial or other civilian traffic to impede military flight training.

These days there's an informal grouping of U.S. military branches in the Nevada and California high deserts—Navy, Marine, Air Force—developing combat flying techniques and providing servicewide training. The group's impact is growing, being felt worldwide. No wonder this bunch has acquired the informal name of the Desert Mafia!

The "Big Five" Desert Mafia Navy members include Strike at Fallon; Top Gun at Miramar; the VX-5 test and experimental squadron at China Lake, which flies F/A-18 Hornets; and its sister squadron VX-4 at Point Mugu. Then there is the Marine Air Warfare Training Squadron One (MAWTS-1) at MCAS Yuma, with direct connections to the Third Marine Air Wing based

---

Previous pages: Trio of Strike faculty aircraft (A-6 in the lead, F/A-18 on left, A-7 on right) pose for photographer Hall against Sierra Nevada backdrop.

at El Toro, south of Los Angeles, but in fact host to Marine aviation worldwide.

Although not an ''official'' Mafia member, don't overlook NAS Whidbey as an activity that, even though on the ocean, up in the Puget Sound area, does lots of A-6/EA-6 overland low-level penetration work. Their attack and ECM (electronic countermeasures) training incorporates routes all over the Columbia River basin in Washington that extend down to NAS Fallon. Other related Navy activities include the attack pukes at Lemoore, who send their F/A-18 RAG (re-placement air group), VFA-125, to Fallon routinely. The Marines also have permanent elements of VFA-106 at Fallon, all the way from Jacksonville's Cecil Field, a Navy RAG that includes USMC students and instructors.

Don't forget the Air Force, either. Because of its abundant airspace, Fallon sees some of

NAS Fallon, burgeoning attack base and home of Strike, displays full and active flight line.

the Air Force's test work from Edwards, plus the ubiquitous Red Flag and Fighter Weapons School training at Nellis, the F-4G Wild Weasel bunch from George. There's even been talk of connecting the military-controlled airspace areas with a Fallon-Nellis corridor, to create what would undoubtedly be the world's single largest range. Currently, though, the planned link is electronic, between Fallon's TACTS (Tactical Air Combat Training System) and the ACMI (air-combat maneuvering instrumentation) at Nellis.

Even the Air Force Reserve F-16s up at Hill AFB in Utah have a role and share evolutions with Strike. Hill's work has become integrated to the extent that missions are flown routinely between ranges and units.

No-holds-barred flying! Yes, indeed. In this respect, Fallon is The Place. This is an area where you can fly and fly and fly, push it to the edge of the envelope and hardly see another soul, unless it's maybe an adversary looking for trouble, briefed to scout the area with malice aforethought in his cunningly camouflaged Aggressor F-16N, F-5E, or A-4 Mongoose, a fighter pilot from almost any Desert Mafia site looking for trouble, who can hardly wait to beat up on your innocent F-14 or F/A-18, your less maneuverable and more vulnerable A-6 or A-7 or—God help you!—some other even lowlier machine.

Innocent? Hardly. If you're saddled up in a military airplane in the Fallon area, on official

Attack three-ship departs Dixie Valley and Bravo-17 target complex.

business, you're prima facie guilty as hell, likely to pay the price. Don't believe? Just wait ten seconds, maybe less.

A violent business at Strike, and throughout the Desert Mafia. As a member of the Strike staff puts it, with a trace of bias: "We control millions of dollars in U.S. government weapons and training programs. I look around the Desert Mafia and see men with vision, dedicated to putting out the best, most accurate gouge on strike warfare in the Navy. We fly like pros . . . we just happen to be tactical warrior pros."

BIRTH STRUGGLE

December 1983. The U.S. Navy, specifically its TACAIR (tactical air) activity, has experienced one of its worst-ever reverses in years, the costly and ineffectual attempt to silence a Syrian IADS (Integrated Air-Defense System) in the Bekáa Valley. Recriminations have passed from office to office at the highest levels, but the bottom line is that the Navy's TACAIR capabilities are in urgent need of help.

Some of the writing went up on the wall during Vietnam. When sixteen Navy fighters had been lost for the destruction of forty enemy aircraft, at a 2.5:1 kill ratio in favor of the United States, the Navy's response was to create Top Gun. Much of the Defense Department's claim to superiority in aerial combat had been based on the

---

Northern Nevada moonscape passes beneath Strike A-7, A-6, and F/A-18.

ability of technologically superior U.S. fighters to beat back the huge numerical advantage of the other side. Seen in this light 2.5:1 was a losing proposition, and everyone knew it. But—and even though the raw numbers are in the books, few outside the business talk about it—at the same time, over the same period, 288 Navy A-1, A-3, A-4, A-6, and A-7 attack birds had been lost. In the case of the strike business, the causes were many and varied, not confined to mano-a-mano ACM (air-combat maneuvering) as with the fighters.

Part of the attack community's response was to create LAWES (Light Attack Weapons Employment School)/PAC at Lemoore, but it was a local A-7 effort and not sponsored at the highest levels. MAWTS-1 at Yuma was also forging ahead, independently, refining its attack work. In the mid-1970s, MAWTS-1 was under the direction of Howard DeCastro, that remarkable Marine aviator and Phantom driver, and winner of the 1973 Cunningham Award for outstanding aviator of the year. Even then the need was evident among thoughtful attack community pilots to create something that would pull it all together.

Capt. Joe Prueher was in a position to know—he was commanding an air wing in the Mediterranean aboard the *Eisenhower,* under Adm. Jerry Tuttle, who would shortly put his experience and will, his heart, soul, and career on the line with such courage and commitment.

Prueher has come off the line in early December with *Ike*'s return to the East Coast and is settling in at NAS Oceana. *JFK* and *Indy* are out in the eastern Mediterranean now, with Jerry Tuttle still running the show. Tensions are high, and although few realize it at the time, the shit is about to hit the fan.

"The December (1983) Lebanon raid crystallized the problem for the attack community, and for the Navy." Joe Prueher speaks with hindsight, but at the time he didn't realize how deeply he would become involved and what an influence Strike was to have on his career.

What has to be done will have to be an inside job. In many ways the military is no different from business, from the social milieu, from politics, from government. You can often do more over a cup of coffee, a beer at the O Club, or a 3:00 A.M. phone call between old friends than in months of official paperwork, via rivers of signals and memoranda, or after endless butt- and mind-numbing meetings in which everyone is jockeying for position and protecting their political flanks and fannies. We're talking budding careers here—or busted ones.

John Lehman, Secretary of the Navy, ends up as the sparkplug of the entire Strike creation, establishing it in Fallon as the eventual linchpin of the Desert Mafia. He is not only SecNav but also a Reserve A-6 B/N who understands the business from the inside, and who has a strong personal interest in straightening out the mess and building for the future.

Lehman energizes his best naval air warfare minds, starting with Adm. Robert "Dutch" Schultz, and his deputy Adm. Ronald Hayes, along with Capt. Bruce Bremner. He tasks them to do some preliminary fact finding. Also involved is Capt. Ray Alcorn, the man who will end up personally assembling the team that will create the reports and recommendations. Looking back on the process, Joe Prueher was to say later, "Lehman's backing, personal insistence, and determination made Strike happen."

Alcorn himself is an interesting character. He was a Vietnam POW for a grim six and a half years, downed on his third mission in the A-4 at the very start of serious hostilities. He has the respect of the TACAIR community as an officer and an aviator who understands the Washington and Pentagon political arenas. He has Connections and he Knows the Good Guys.

The grapevine starts to buzz and the calls start

In the weeds: F/A-18 Hornet heads in at 400 knots, 100 feet.

"Loneliest road in America" slices through Dixie Valley range complex.

to go out. The brains being pulsed will—it is hoped—reveal the real roots of TACAIR's problems in the Mediterranean, so that solutions can be developed.

One of the individuals involved is stockbroker Roger Whiteway, a former A-6 driver still flying weekends in the Reserve. Whiteway is starting to hit his stride, the financial big time. He's been earning good money for his clients—mostly Active and Reserve Navy. They trust him and his judgment, for good reason. With his high energy level, his discipline, and his analytical mind, Roger Whiteway is good at what he does. No, he is excellent.

Strike's needs will be many: money and management, certainly, but also a whole lot of advanced technology. What, asks Bruce Bremner,

does Roger think should be done about Strike's technological end, wherever it may be located? Could he, by chance, jot down some thoughts, the beginnings of a plan? Roger Whiteway cannot easily shake off the business that has consumed him all the way from college into his thirties. He has been asked for an opinion. He will deliver one.

The following morning Roger Whiteway gets up at 5:00 A.M., unable to sleep, goes to his PC in the den wearing just his bathrobe, and starts to peck out a plan. He has a fine analytical mind—after all, he has that Ph.D. in mechanical engineering, in fluid-flow dynamics, which the Navy helped him get. He has a way with words as well as with numbers. And he is interested— no, he is passionately involved—in the attack world.

Unfettered by any sort of official restrictions, and writing unclassified material on a private PC, he starts to describe his Dream Attack Range, the sort of place he'd build and the technological tools he'd install if money were no impediment, if he could get support for his ideas.

What he doesn't realize is that this is pretty much how it will turn out! And that far from being just a sounding board, an outside and disinterested observer, a Reserve who is now safely out of the loop, he will soon be in it up to his neck or deeper.

The basic conclusion of all this activity is that a complete, integrated attack community training system must be created. It should include, as a bare minimum, a range with full electronic and computational aids that will offer every type of ground and air target and threat, test and exercise every type of capability an air wing could possess or might need to work with as the asset of some other group, and have the innate flexibility to grow into the future—a long-range future in a dangerous world.

But who will run the show? Getting off to the right start will determine the future effectiveness of the activity. From the point of view of Navy top management, all the way up to the Chief of Naval Operation's office where Serious Decisions are made, the need is for people, the very best men they can find. Jerry Tuttle has been monitoring the proceedings from the start, and he supplies a short list of names to OP-05, names of officers he'd consider for skipper at Strike. One of the names on that list is that of Joe Prueher, settling back into his flying work at Oceana, actually involved in a FFARP (Fleet Fighter ACM Readiness Program) evolution with VF-142 at Oceana. Ray Alcorn has said all along that appointing a CO is top priority.

Around the end of April 1984 Admiral Hayes calls Joe Prueher and asks him to take over Strike. He sells well, explaining to Prueher how valuable the effort, a training system that will embody all the elements of mission planning, will be.

The system will have to include every critical support element a theater commander might need—current and complete intelligence, every ordnance load air wing aircraft might carry, EW (electronic warfare) and ASW (antisubmarine warfare) capabilities, computer support systems for mission planning, the ability to undertake detailed contingency plans against virtually all operational eventualities, CSAR (combat search-and-rescue) briefs, and the relationship between air wing activity and all other fleet elements in the area. Everything but the kitchen sink.

After all, as Hayes explains, we're going to train complete air wings and CAGs (command-

Fake airfield target (*top right*) catches attention of attacking A-7 Corsair.

ers, air group), and they are the tip of the spear in the event of hostilities, the very essence of power projection anywhere in the world, most especially places where only carrier battle groups can go because there are no accessible land bases. With all the current emphasis on nuclear disarmament, on reduced strategic deterrence, the role of Navy tactical power projection will become increasingly important, that much is clear. No other U.S. military activity, Prueher realizes, has that mission, that sort of scope, that breadth of real responsibility.

In the meantime Whiteway sends his technology report to Bremner, who forwards it to Alcorn. As far as Whiteway is concerned, the subject is closed and he can devote his attention to his existing customers and to the estate of a client,

Strike A-6 Intruder unfolds wings before instructional hop.

a retired schoolteacher who sold her farm in southern Virginia to a developer and netted millions. For Whiteway, this last project alone will represent a major effort, six-figure earnings. The professional coup of a lifetime. He reckons without Joe Prueher.

Prueher has the reputation of being a winner and picking winners, and he is getting the pick of the crop in naval aviation—the sort of folks who'd never be caught dead in a place like Fallon unless it was a sound career move. He shakes

his own trees and starts to build his team—a team of certified winners.

The group gets together for a kickoff meeting at Lemoore. It includes his XO, Comdr. Bill ''Bear'' Pickavance, who until Joe called was XO of the *Connie;* Lt. Comdr. Dave Nichols, an A-6 NFO who will end up as tactics leader at Strike; Comdr. ''Stretch'' McKenzie, a Tom-cat driver and XO of VF-192 who will manage coordination; and an electronicker, Lt. Comdr. John Ross, out of the EA-6B community at Whidbey, who will assemble the ground syllabus. ''These were the men who were key in launching Strike and helping us stand up with our best feet forward,'' says Prueher.

The gouge has gone out throughout the entire Navy TACAIR community, and anyone with an ounce of brains knows that something big is happening there and that it's time to get in on the action. Who has the plan?

The plan. Yes, indeed, Prueher has a plan, based significantly on OP-05's staff work, the fruits of that Lemoore meeting, and the original hacking Whiteway has done on his PC at home. It makes your average fast track look slow.

By the end of April 1984 Prueher says that Strike can deliver its first SLATS (Strike Leader Attack Training Syllabus) course in October. They have had less than six months to create a full, working program and execute it. If it is done well they may survive. If it isn't . . . well, after all, daily life in military aviation has always been a high-stakes personal game of bet your career and your assets.

What about a name? What would you call the joint? It would probably be called, as suggested by SecNav, the CNO staff, and others involved, something akin to the name the fighter community has given to the Navy's Fighter Weapons School for ACM—Top Gun. The words Top Bomb appeared on someone's memorandum, but there is something wrong with that, something not fully formed. For the moment it will have to be formal: Naval Strike Warfare Center (NSWC), or something like that.

The right place for all this? Well, it is offered first of all to China Lake, but they refuse it. Then the decision is made to locate at Fallon, where the Navy already has a foot on the scorched ground. NAS Fallon. The decision is made eventually in Washington. The China Lake bunch suddenly realize that the deal is serious and try to reopen the subject, but by then it is too late. Fallon will be the place. Of course no one in his right mind would actually go there himself.

Prueher and Pickavance have another problem beyond busting butt with twelve-hour days and seven-day weeks to get the physical plant ready, recruit a staff of superstars, and prepare lectures for that first class in October. The problem is that of appointing a technical director to run the scientific end of things. Prueher has advertised for civilian candidates qualified with the right academic and strike-leader experience, but no one materializes. He has called Roger Whiteway from time to time, asking for advice but really trolling for a good candidate (Roger himself), but Whiteway has tactfully explained about his new career. Anyway, the best Prueher can offer is a GM-15 slot, paying a piddling $50,000.

Dr. Roger Whiteway, the Reserve A-6 pilot and stockbroker welded to the ground in Virginia, is at a crossroads. He thinks about it for a long time, fighting the conflicts of a career that will make him independent compared with a return to a life that will make overwhelming technical and physical demands on him and cost him—realistically—huge amounts of financial reward. Finally he says what the hell, calls Prueher, and accepts the more challenging future. All he has to do now is telephone all his clients and tell them that he's leaving the stockbroking business.

Fall 1984. Dr. Roger Whiteway, newly appointed technical director to the freshly minted Naval Strike Warfare Center, steps off the plane in Reno on 26 September 1984 and finds it hard to accept what he is experiencing. It is so hot that it is hard to breathe. The sun has a harsh, brittle quality that seems to illuminate the bones—X rays in the visible part of the spectrum. His PC hadn't warned him about all this. He had conveniently blotted out the secondhand memories of Fallon.

He had resigned as an A-6 pilot in the regular Navy after thirteen hard years, part of a promise to his wife that settling down in Virginia, buying a house, and raising kids were the top priority. This foolishness with military aviation would be out of his system—except for those Reserve weekends, that is.

He looks around at the violent and rocky ridges and pinnacles of the Sierra Nevada to the west. He remembers that as a regular A-6 pilot in an East Coast squadron, he had managed through some stroke of good luck to avoid being sent to NAS Fallon even as TAD (temporarily assigned duty). He realizes now how lucky he was. And he is still in Reno, in civilization . . . of a sort. He hasn't even taken that god-awful trek sixty miles to the east yet! Just to think that he has volunteered for this, changing his entire life!

Now, with official SecNav approval and the appropriate blessings and initial funding, they have forged a team and an operation that is starting to get real results. The foot-dragging skeptics in Washington are coming around, and finally visitors, all the way to flag rank and including all the essential senior civilian scientists and bureaucrats, are coming to that misbegotten Fallon to see for themselves where all their money is going. Turn on the air conditioning, guys—the admiral is on his way.

Finally a name comes down that sticks. Leh-

NSWC ORGANIZATIONAL CHART JANUARY 1988

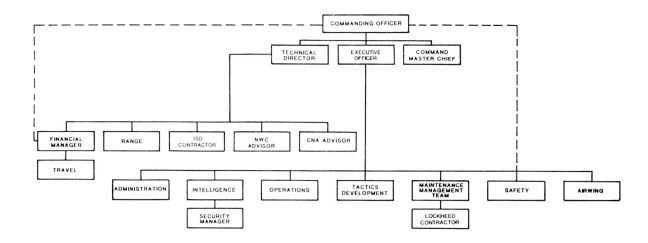

man wants to call it Strike University, which is immediately shortened to the blunt and business-like form Strike.

Progress is visible. There are buildings, an old hangar, a staff of 25 officers and 32 enlisted, eight aircraft for the Strike staff to fly, and the grudging respect of the attack community. Secure at Fallon, Strike has established itself as the Navy power projection capital. The workload has been awesome, the hours long, but the product now speaks for itself. Joe Prueher's staff of hand-picked officers has been given both responsibility and authority to find, evaluate, and solve naval air-warfare problems. Now they are in demand from all major commands and can provide view-points and information without the taint of paro-chialism.

They cannot anticipate it at the time, but in two full years of operation, all sixteen of the Navy's Active (fourteen) and Reserve (two) air wings will have been to Strike at least once, including those East and West Coast Reserve air wings whose capabilities were significantly enhanced through Lehman's initiatives and urgings. Over 1,000 officers will have attended SLATS, receiving the most up-to-date information to help them lead coordinated strikes. Strike is on the map, getting results.

NATO is paying attention. By summer of 1987 there are three West German Panavia Tornado aircraft parked on the flight line at Fallon, and a bunch of (inevitably) rowdy West German pilots and backseaters in the O Club bar. Many nations have had the chance to savor the delights of Red Flag. Can Strike be far behind, with the reasonable competition between Navy and Air Force?

At the heart of air wing training at Strike is the world's biggest and most sophisticated video system, Fallon's single largest nonflying techno-logical investment. Officially dubbed TACTS, or Tactical Air Combat Training System, it is a $25 million adult computer game that pilots get to play with if they're good. And if they're not so hot, Strike wants to bring 'em up to speed.

Although TACTS is the technological heart of Strike's air wing training programs, there is a broad choice of range capabilities, covering five separate geographical sites and accompany-ing MOAs (military operating areas) on the local aviation charts that offer varying features to the Strike training and planning staffs:

- **Bravo 16** is a conventional or special-weapons bombing range close enough to NAS Fallon to be suitable for short (thirty- to forty-five-minute) sorties. Video scoring (via a set of remotely controlled cameras) is used to measure weapon impacts.

- **Bravo 17** (see map) is the largest and most elaborate of the Fallon ranges, established in the Dixie Valley south of U.S. Highway 50 for most conventional strike objectives. The Bravo 17 range includes areas where runways, aircraft, missile sites, POL (petroleum, oil, lu-bricants) storage facilities, and even ''towns'' have been placed in the desert as targets for real and simulated bombing attacks (it was from a hill high atop Bravo 17 range that much of the spectacular ground-to-air photo footage in the movie *Top Gun* was shot). Construction was sponsored and overseen by Strike.

- **Bravo 19** is a multifunction range characterized by deep canyons that cut through the mountains, with roads winding through the area on which simulated vehicle convoys can be placed. This range is used for CAS (close air-support) training or convoy interdiction, using FACs (forward air controllers) on the ground or in the air to call targets and measure results.

- **Bravo 20** is Fallon's live-ordnance range, under development beyond its earlier role, in which no observation or accuracy measurements were made, to a new status in which remote monitoring stations are being installed.

- **Echo Whiskey** range—Echo Whiskey for electronic warfare, naturally—was particularly useful, and used, during the Vietnam conflict and has just been updated at great cost to make it match the latest electronic threats that wing pilots might face in a real IADS environment. The simple and unavoidable fact—in reality, simplicity is not one of the virtues of modern war—is that the electronic-threat environment is escalating faster than the weaponry threat, and Echo Whiskey range reflects this painful reality.

TACTS capabilities extend to much of the range area but are also being upgraded and expanded to provide monitoring capabilities further to the east. This has become essential—the eastern extremities are marked by a series of north-south mountain ranges that have become, over the years, highly popular with ingressing sorties as good places to hide. Pilots who have been to Strike have come to know rather well the

Strike trio sucks it in for bad-to-the-bone break formation over Fallon runway.

NAS FALLON RANGES AND AIRSPACE

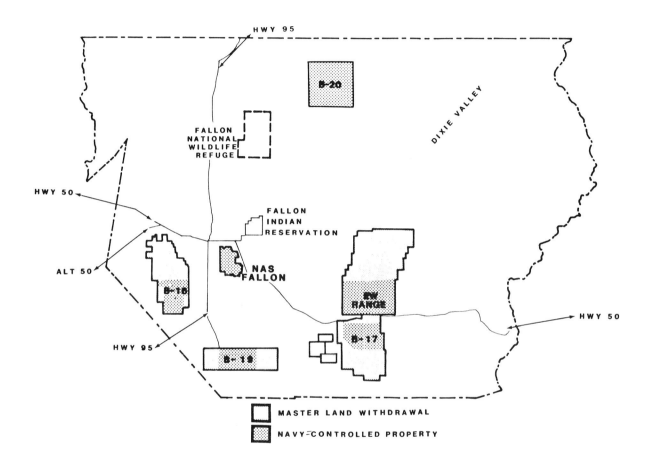

existing surveillance limitations.

The Dixie Valley controversy seems to be a permanent feature of the Fallon political landscape. Dixie Valley is in the heart of the Bravo 17 range, and it has been the center of more than just aerial activity since the Fallon facilities started their modernization in the early 1980s. This is an area where the targets will be set up, data links and other high-cost pieces of technology installed at key sites on mountaintops.

Impossible to ignore, the controversy has also been the focus of some continuing, unfriendly exchanges between the Navy and the local ranchers, some of whom have been concerned with the way in which aircraft and possibly weapons have been used in the area. Goodwill on both

BRAVO 17
TACTICAL TARGET COMPLEX

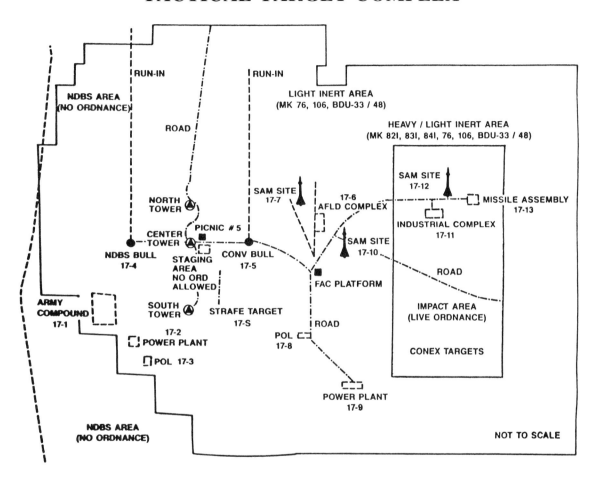

sides—reasonable men and women doing the best they can with the situation—has been strained to the limit. Dixie Valley is now under review as the heart of a proposed supersonic range area that will permit visiting wing aircraft to exceed the speed of sound, with the inevitable sonic-boom results.

One thing is sure: the Desert Mafia is here to stay. Range capabilities and activities will escalate as the need for authentic, advanced training in all the possible worldwide attack scenarios grows, as the United States and its allies face potential adversaries who far outspend them in military defense and export yearly. There is no going back. The American people deserve nothing less than the best.

Painful Lessons

"Sacrifices must be made."

—Reputed last words of flying pioneer Otto Lilienthal before plunging to his death in an early experimental glider

14 November 1910.   Civilian pilot Eugene Ely is about to make history, one way or the other. He is not sure how it will go— either he will demonstrate a "first," flight from a ship's deck, or he may suffer serious injury or death. He adopts a studied nonchalance that he does not feel as he completes the final walk-around of his flimsy Curtiss pusher biplane, testing the soundness of the wire rigging and fittings, checking the controls, ensuring that engine oil leaks are down to the acceptable minimum.

From his vantage point on the specially rigged eighty-three-foot-long platform on the fo'c'sle of the cruiser USS *Birmingham* at Hampton Roads, Virginia, he can look down and see the upturned faces of the sailors as they silently watch him complete his preparations. This will be a day to remember, for them and—with any luck— for himself. He does not realize it, does not even think about it, but today he will become immortal.

18 January 1911.   The San Francisco morning is bright but cool as Ely's Curtiss pusher lifts off from the runway at Crissy Field and banks over the empty straits between San Francisco and Marin County to the north. At his 500-foot cruising altitude he descries the cruiser

Pennsylvania, ploughing through the Bay waters into a moderate westerly breeze that will work in his favor.

That flight back last November was not a fluke, he tells himself. It was a glimpse of the future. He and his supporters back at the Navy Department in Washington are sure that the ship can be made into a more powerful and effective weapon by adding air power. But their many skeptics are vocal, downright derisive, despite the early success of the program.

Ely turns his aircraft east, downwind, watching the *Pennsylvania,* then swings back to align himself astern. Across the 120-foot quarterdeck he can make out the wires, attached to sandbags, that will—if he is lucky—arrest his landing progress. It is straight up 1100. As Ely makes his final approach he thinks of Navy Lt. T. G. Ellyson, who is planning a catapult launch from a ship's deck as soon as possible.

18 April 1942.   It is just before dawn in the western Pacific. A misty overcast softens the foam-flecked sea. U.S. Army Air Corps Lt. Col. James H. Doolittle strides the wooden flight deck of the U.S. carrier *Hornet.* He is still not used to the way the deck pitches and heaves under the influence of those huge Pacific swells. He is a soldier, an airman perhaps, not a sailor. No, he is a warrior and so are his companions, all of them fighting in a common cause, Navy and Army Air Corps, regardless of the differences in uniforms and insignia.

Previous pages: At MAWTS-1, Marine Lt. Col. Kevin "KO" O'Mara, 3,000-hour fighter/attack veteran, rolls in with Mark 82s on Chocolate Mountains target in aging VMFA-531 F-4N.

Strike birds head up through winter Nevada overcast.

He stands at last on the bow and looks west, toward Tokyo, feeling in his face the wind caused by the ship's fifteen-knot progress, added to the twenty-two knots generated by the local weather. He turns aft. In the dawn's early light he can make out the stark, brutal outlines of his sixteen B-25 bombers as they sit ready, chocked, lashed to the deck, fully fueled, and loaded with bombs.

He is aware that the Navy would like to undertake this attack but has no suitable airplanes for strategic strikes. In fact, he realizes, power projection from carriers has not yet achieved credibil-

ity. In the last four months, Navy pilots have fought ferociously and heroically in tactical actions throughout the western Pacific. To Doolittle, they are comrades in arms.

He calculates the odds of surviving his mission, going over those implacable numbers in his head for the hundredth time, and decides for the hundredth time that the probability of living out the day is poor, both for him and for his companions. But he also knows that it is time to carry the war to the enemy, a warning to the Japanese that the infamy of four months ago, on 7 December 1941, will be avenged. But unlike the 7 December attack on Pearl Harbor from carriers close enough to be detected, his attack will be from long range—so long, in fact, that he will not be able to return to the carrier but will continue to China and try to find a landing place there. His B-25s are not equipped, anyway, for carrier recovery. They were loaded by crane back in Pearl Harbor.

Jimmy Doolittle sets his face, mindful that he will be watched carefully by everyone around him—by his Navy hosts, by his own men—and that the slightest hint of doubt or concern on his part could be contagious. At heart he is a warrior.

4 December 1983. Rear Adm. Jerry O. Tuttle is a short, feisty man of strong will and persuasive disposition. He has risen to his current rank based on ability, guts, and the usual dash of good luck, being in the right place at the right time, not having any major catastrophes in his record. Tuttle is used to being in charge, taking control, running the show. He commands the two carrier battle groups of the U.S. Sixth Fleet.

Tuttle knows he is standing atop a pinnacle of seventy years' successful Navy experience with carrier operations—in the Atlantic and Pacific in WWII, in Korea, and in Vietnam—seventy years that started back in Hampton Roads, Virginia, in 1911. He is, he knows, simply the latest in an unbroken line of Navy men, going all the way back to John Paul Jones, who have the conn and must make decisions, give orders,

take responsibility. He accepts his destiny.

Tuttle has at his disposal the air wings of *Kennedy* and *Independence,* over 150 aircraft that include F-14 Tomcat fighters, A-6 Intruder and A-7 Corsair attack aircraft, and an array of supporting systems ranging from the E-2C Hawkeye airborne early-warning aircraft to the EA-6B Prowler jammer. There are fixed-wing S-3 Vikings and SH-3 Sea King helicopters for distant and close-in antisubmarine patrol, KA-6 and KA-7 tankers, and EA-3B Whales for sniffing out various enemy electronic activities.

"Give us the tools and we'll finish the job"— Winston Churchill, 1946, Tuttle recalls. Jerry Tuttle has the tools—awesome firepower, superbly trained and motivated men in every position from deck to cockpit—but the command structure apparently won't let him do the job, at least not as he would like. His every plan and order must traverse a lengthy chain of command that extends all the way back to Germany and thence to Washington. The theater commander in Germany is an Army general whose staff seems to have limited appreciation of carrier operations.

He is facing what he regards as a major problem with the proposed punitive strike, intended to teach the Syrians in Lebanon a lesson they will never forget, a lesson that will persuade them to mend their violent ways, to desist from firing on U.S. aircraft overflying for simple reconnaissance, and from using their incessant terrorist tactics. After months on station in the eastern Mediterranean, flogging his men and his aircraft to the limits of their endurance, preparing and then having to abort mission after mission, strike after strike, he has received specific instructions to attack.

The problem, greatly oversimplified, is not enough time to brief and arm his aircraft. The command structure wants a TOT (time over target) of 0730 local, but Tuttle—and his staff, to a man—knows that the 0730 TOT is wrong, wrong, wrong.

At 0730 the morning sun will be coming up behind the hills east of the target, in the face of the incoming attack, and those hills will cast long shadows that will obscure vital target features, make ID impossibly difficult for his pilots and crews. That low morning sun will be focused directly into the canopies of his incoming aircraft, into the eyes of his crews, compounding their problems. Canopies, however carefully cleaned, become scratched over time. Those scratches diffuse and diffract light impinging on them at shallow angles.

It's the worst possible time to launch his strike force. To launch at 0630–0700 for an 0730 TOT,

Navy Aggressor pilot and Marine backseater ready their TA-4 for adversary hop.

he should have begun briefing and arming his air wings starting not later than 0300. Final word did not come through from Washington until much later, around 0430. The administrative and logistical challenges are monumental. Final target planning and staff briefings took him until 0530, and the process was rushed in a way he found quite unacceptable.

At 0530, with insufficient time for full aircrew briefing and aircraft arming, the chosen warplanes are not properly prepared. Tuttle does not know all the details—he has too much to do as it is—but he is aware that some of those A-6 and A-7 attack aircraft are not fully armed with all the appropriate ordnance.

The physical realities of trying to energize the magazines, located in the bowels of the ship for safety, behind massive armor and a complex flash-proof hoist system, are such that it takes more than mere minutes to get it right and arm with precisely the right types of ordnance on the right aircraft. Rearm later? *Not* an option . . .

Other questions assail Tuttle's team, a matrix of detail and decision that always seems, in hindsight, so simple. Many aspects are simply beyond his control, his command purview. It has to be a U.S. thrust, without involving allies. But should the USS *New Jersey* be used, that monstrous battleship with its sixteen-inch guns, to pound those enemy sites, or is this too remote and imprecise a presence, risking civilian casualties? Should a small, skilled, and dedicated team of U.S. Navy SEALS be sent ashore with the right kind of explosives, to perform destructive microsurgery, or would this be seen by a critical world as a form of insurgency, terrorism of the kind

the United States so strongly opposes? Must it be an air strike? What is the right answer?

It is impossible for Tuttle to know it all from his position aboard the flagship in the eastern Mediterranean. He is a great warrior and a loyal one, and he is sure that all the right questions have been asked by all the right people in all the right places. Or . . . have they? He knows by first name most of the Navy men involved, has for years, but few of the others except those in his direct chain of command.

Tuttle is a warrior, not a statesman or a politician or a diplomat, but he knows that the position of the United States in the world is endlessly at stake, always under scrutiny, often under attack. Whatever he does or is told to do, he will shortly be at the focal point of world affairs, painfully visible.

Then there is the enemy. The enemy is determined not to let those American devils come in, those Americans with their battle group of aircraft carriers and cruisers and destroyers and frigates and support ships that has been sitting off Lebanon for months, a grey floating city of potential death, threatening them daily in the air and at sea. Those Americans, with their arrogance, their public contempt for Arabs, whom they have the effrontery to call "ragheads." If they do come, if they dare, a price will have to be paid, extracted in American blood. The Syrians are prepared, ready.

Another part of the problem Tuttle faces, beyond timing, is the modern IADS—Integrated Air-Defense System. The Syrians in the Bekáa Valley have been equipped with an IADS, devised by the Soviets, consisting of every form of aerial unpleasantness. There are AAA (antiaircraft artillery) and SAMs (surface-to-air missiles), all under the control of radar linked to computers, a fully integrated defense that can make life hell for incoming attack aircraft. This is the same IADS that has been firing repeatedly on his TARPS-equipped F-14 Tomcats doing high-speed aerial photoreconnaissance, although no serious damage has been inflicted on them—yet.

Tuttle is a careful and painstaking executive, responsible for billions of dollars' worth of taxpayers' assets, thousands of lives. He does not take his job lightly, working over twenty hours a day. He wants to know a lot more about the situation, but there are intelligence gaps that he has been unable to fill despite his most persuasive and persistent efforts up and down the chain of command. He needs to know more about what is happening on the ground in the target area and around it. He would like to know all about the information that has passed between the Syrians in Lebanon and their Communist supporters, to see whether the enemy is weakening or has other hostile intentions beyond his immediate tactical scope.

He needs facts to work on, to use as essential planning elements, but good and complete intelligence is lacking. And the rules of engagement, the limitations placed on targets, remind him of the restrictions that bedeviled him in 'Nam years ago.

All in all, it is shaping up to be a bad scene. He knows it intellectually, and he feels it in his gut. There is little upside opportunity, much downside risk. Tuttle is a remarkably capable man, a courageous warrior, but he understands that he must take as well as give orders. His air wing commanders know it, and so do his aircrews. This is what they signed on for. Tuttle orders the attack to proceed as ordered. Into the Bekáa Valley of Death.

17 December 1983. Navy Secretary John Lehman sits in his office alone, his Pentagon desk illuminated by a single lamp. It is 3:00 A.M., but he has not yet gone home or eaten dinner. He is reviewing the classified signals and analyses accumulated from the Sixth Fleet, Chief of Naval Operations, Joint Chiefs of Staff, the White House. Subject: the Bekáa Valley debacle. Two aircraft lost, one man killed, another taken prisoner, the U.S. Navy attack community—of which, as a Reserve A-6 B/N, he is an integral part—disgraced and discredited in the eyes of many. Not to put too fine a point on it, someone has screwed up. There has been much finger pointing, many evasions, no firm conclusions.

Lehman, the aggressive, ambitious SecNav, hates to admit it, but he is exhausted and a bit discouraged. It is 3:00 A.M., but this won't wait. He sets his paperwork down, rubs his eyes, runs his hands over his face, feels his almost twenty-four-hour growth of stubble. He pulls out his billfold, takes out his diary, flicks rapidly through the names and addresses of key men to call.

It is time, he decides, to take the initiative, to grasp the opportunity, to assimilate the lessons that he has just been taught through the reading of all these depressing signals. There must be a way to reverse this sort of problem, use it as a learning experience, a fresh start, a means for the attack community to change and grow. If he, the Secretary of the Navy, cannot find and implement the solutions, who can?

Mission:
The Inside Gouge

"Graduate level training for strike leaders is needed to ensure that the (U.S.) Navy is second to none in power projection."

—Strike's Capt. Robert G. Brodsky quoted in *Tail Hook*

"Our mission? We're here to train the Navy TACAIR air wings and strike leaders for maximum effectiveness in tactical strike warfare missions, anywhere in the world."

He says it, up front. Capt. Robert G. "Bubba" Brodsky, U.S. Navy, a trim forty-five years old in 1988, is the third Strike skipper since operations started in 1985, after Capt. Joe Prueher (April 1984 to February 1986) and Capt. Jay Finney (February 1986 to May 1987). Brodsky is expected to leave in late 1988 to take a new job as a senior air group commander.

Brodsky is stating his basic role as a warrior, keeper of the flame, teacher of warriors. He makes his case without apology, in a world and a time that have come increasingly to see warriors as outcasts, unclassifiable and potentially dangerous, despite the fact that the nation elected Dwight Eisenhower to the presidency after WWII. The world has changed.

Brodsky is tall and fit, with a suntanned and serious face creased much of the time by a big smile. Not that he is other than a serious man; he just clearly feels his life and his work with intensity. Those emotions include joy and pleasure in what he is doing, flying and managing

---

Previous pages: Look out below! A-7 Corsair with Zuni rockets in wing pods rolls in for attack over Dixie Valley range.

Strike, at the pinnacle of a successful career.

Brodsky treats visitors with close attention and complete courtesy. There are few interruptions. Despite his uniform khakis, it's easier to picture him in his "bag" in the briefing room, getting ready to walk down and put his pork on the line in an A-6 or A-7 as he has done so often, including Vietnam. In fact, he spends half his time in a bag, ready to fly, flying, or right back from a hop. Flying is his life. As for so many flyers, it has been so for Bubba since he was a kid.

First, Brodsky explains the status and command relationships of Strike in more detail: "Organizationally, Strike works for the CNO. Our operational Navy (OPNAV) sponsor is the Deputy Chief of Naval Operations, Air Warfare, back in the Pentagon, commonly referred to as 'OP-05.'" In 1987–88 OP-05 was Vice Adm. Robert F. Dunn, a former attack pilot. It doesn't hurt to have a sponsor from your own community.

Because of the way we were established, with the direct approval and support of the Secretary of the Navy, we have had a lot of latitude, almost a free hand in how we related to the rest of the Navy.

We're allowed direct liaison with fleet commanders in chief, with the numbered fleets, type commanders, the various Navy labs around the country, the test and evaluation (T&E) squadrons, carrier air wings, and units of the other U.S. armed forces agencies, the Marines, the Air Force, and the Army.

All three—and a number of other groups as well—have plenty of responsibility and experience in tactical aviation and lots of good ideas about how to do it better. We have a lot to learn, but as a visitor sees after spending a little time around here, there's little (in the attack area) we don't try to get into, one way or another.

NEW ERA IN TACTICAL WARFARE

Brodsky continues: *Tactical warfare today has entered a new era. It has become increasingly complex—the days of just strapping on an airplane and driving off to move mud, drop bombs on the bad guys, are gone forever.*

The Navy is good at learning lessons and paying attention to finding the right answers and applying them. Remember our poor 2.5:1 (Navy: enemy) kill ratio in the early days of Vietnam? It led to the creation of Top Gun. For Strike, our stimulus was similar: Lebanon 1983. An obvious deficiency existed . . .

Lebanon taught us a painful lesson. But from where I sit we've picked up on that experience, as well as others that have come along around the world, and put them to work in a positive

Frustrated tank driver (and Strike skipper) Capt. Bob ''Bubba'' Brodsky gets strangely excited at controls of Sgt. York/DIVAD antiaircraft ground-crawler.

A-7 attack bird slings captive Sidewinder air-to-air missile for ACM training.

sense. That's why Strike was formed, and that's why it's working. Everyone, all the way up the line, has a stake in making this place go right. They're giving us the support we need.

Our task is to make sure that fleet aviation commanders are kept fully abreast of tactical developments and other matters of tactical importance as they arise, both in overland strike and war-at-sea tactical development. Strike is quite simply tasked to be the Navy's prime authority for aviation strike tactics. That means we must gather the knowledge, keep it current, and then develop demonstrably effective training techniques.

Brodsky is an attack pilot by training and experience, recent past commander of an air group (CAG). He is Strike's man on the spot at Fallon, where his activity is a tenant of the naval air station, commanded in 1988 by Capt. Ray Al-

Attack puke's view of the world: TA-7 two-seater rolls over the vertical to hammer a ground target.

corn—the same man who had been in Washington and had reviewed the original proposals that led to Strike's creation.

We are tasked to perform numerous missions and functions. The mission sounds relatively straightforward. In reality it's complex. It can be much more complicated than, say, Top Gun, which is primarily concerned with air-to-air superiority. This is not to take anything away from the truly outstanding job done elsewhere, but strike warfare invokes virtually every capability in a carrier battle group, and a lot more.

Most people outside the attack community can't picture the level of detail involved in the attack community's business in the late 1980s. "Part of our problem is that the threat changes all the time," explains Brodsky. He understates.

That threat evolution seems to be accelerating! For us it means providing training that antici-

33

pates what is coming along and providing training and tactics that will meet and beat the other guy. We must initiate, not just respond. If we don't react, it could be too late. We do a lot of listening and learning throughout the aerospace community and within the Desert Mafia. And although we don't always tell 'em, we learn—lots—from every wing that comes to town!

In practice this means that we must cover more than a score of subjects in the formal syllabus, all the way from the individual weapons our strike aircraft carry to the broadest possible scope of potential targets and how to get at them. We have to present our material at more than one level, from overviews for nonaviation staff officers down to the nitty-gritty for wing aviators.

Air-to-surface weapons get top priority. "The latest air-to-surface weapons we carry have become very sophisticated," explains Brodsky. We drop iron bombs, of course—500-pound Mark

Iron mayhem: Mark-82 500-pound practice bombs. Blue paint always signifies inert ordnance.

82s as the typical example. But then we have laser-guided bombs, TV-guided weapons, ordnance using IR [infrared] sensors such as FLIR [forward-looking infrared] for target acquisition, air-launched decoy vehicles, the Harpoon in all its variants. And we mesh tactics with Tomahawk—a surface- or subsurface-launched cruise missile that can be equipped either with conventional or nuclear warheads.

Intelligence runs a close second. *Intelligence has become an increasingly important consideration. It used to be—in the bad old days—that you'd go to your intel guy and he'd look embarrassed and tell you that he hated to say it but you weren't cleared with the right security classification to see his stuff. Then he'd . . . close his office door. Remember, this is the guy who was supposedly working for you!*

"Today, well, it works a little better." Brodsky smiles, and you know he's been there. *We're staffed with high-level intel pros. They have created a large intel database and library, and we can get virtually real-time data to an air wing on essentially any subject in any location around the world. Difficulties with the security system have gone away, reflecting top-level recognition of the tactical aviator's real 'need-to-know' situation.*

Brodsky reflects much of the Lehman-era spirit prevalent throughout TACAIR. For many in both the attack and fighter communities, it was a long time coming.

Comdr. Patrick ("Pat") Doyle runs the tactics department at Strike. Lt. Comdr. Bill ("Dawg") Shepherd also provided many enormously helpful inputs and coordinated many questions and requests for further data. Dawg is an old Desert

Real Mark-82s this time. A-7 carries quartet of 500-pound mudthumpers.

Mafia hand, with almost 1,000 hours of Hornet time at Lemoore and China Lake, almost a walking encyclopedia of knowledge about the airframe, as well as the source of inside gouge on Strike.

"Some of us," recalls Pat, "can recall the 'good old days,' when a wing detachment [DET] to Fallon meant lots of good flying, throwing money away at the crap tables in town, and hitting Lake Tahoe on weekends." You just know that Doyle's had his share of Fallon DETs.

The better part of the two-week DET was spent getting aircrews and squadrons up to speed, completing competitive exercise [COMPEX] events, and holding wing bombing/fighter derbies. In the waning days of the DET, CAG would assemble an alpha strike for a trip through the

EW range en route to Bravo 17 for a coordinated strike. Debrief? First one to the chalkboard or the bar won. Exaggeration? Yes, but not by much.

Today, at Strike, we are the central coordinator for developing and executing comprehensive air wing training programs, tasked to coordinate support services, provide ground academics, develop strike scenarios, help strike planners, and establish an air wing training database. The only caveat to the CNO's tasking was that it should not take away CAG's responsibility to train his wing.

We integrate air wing tactical capabilities using a building-block approach, moving from basic to complex scenarios. Each training program includes all the appropriate hardware, tactics, and threat presentations, on a time frame from now to about eighteen months after the DET at Strike.

SLATS

Slats. Leading-edge lift devices, right? That whimsy was in *Aimpoint*, the naval strike warfare review, volume 1, issue 1 (unclassified). To Strike, the acronym stands for the primary integration tool, available in at least two forms for essentially all levels and categories of Navy activity relating in any way to power projection:

Hornet in full attack mode: 500-pound bomb and Zuni rocket pods adorn wing stations.

SLATS—Strike Leader Attack Training Syllabus, basically a ten-day academic course on the weapons, tactics, and integrated naval air warfare.

SLATS is designed for operational and staff officers. In the words of Joe Prueher's first SLATS course manager, Lt. Comdr. Doug Undesser: "Attendees quickly put aside coast and community parochialism." A miracle?

SLATS comes full blown and as X-SLATS (executive level, primarily for battle group commanders and their staffs). SLATS's syllabus covers weapons and "weaponeering," strike-support assets, full intel support, planning aspects, lessons learned from prior conflicts (e.g., Lebanon, Libya, the Falklands), and threat systems and tactics. For best results, four approaches are used: the conventional classroom, group discussions, strike-planning seminars, and strike exercises. The course covers two full weeks and is presented at Fallon six times a year independently of wing visits.

The SLATS course is intensive. It is designed to challenge and improve the prowess of highly motivated senior officers, wing strike leaders, and carrier staff strike planners. Strike has room for just fifty-four officers at each SLATS course, and it's a valuable item in any personnel folder.

For its course openings at each SLATS, Strike has established quotas by activity, background, and experience. You wouldn't send just anyone to a SLATS course. There is a preferred mix of backgrounds and responsibilities, not only between areas of work but in terms of operational

---

Typical SLATS attendance profile

Activity	Atlantic	Pacific
VAM (Medium-attack, A-6)	4	4
VAL/VFA (Light-attack/Strike fighter, A-7, F/A-18)	6	6
VF (Fighter community, F-14)	3	3
VAW (AEW, E-2Cs)	2	2
VS/HS (S-3s, H-3s)	1	1
VAQ (Electronic warfare, EA-6B)	0	2
CVW OPS (Air wing ops)	2	2
CV/CVW AI (CVW/Wing intel)	2	2
CV STK OPS (Ship/Strike)	2	2
CVBG AIR OPS/STK OPS	2	2
CV-ASST CIC (Combat info)	2	2
Subtotals	26	28
Totals	54	

geography (East Coast or West Coast).

The chart provides a view of the typical SLATS mix.

WING DETACHMENTS TO STRIKE

Effective attack work, says current wisdom, comes from understanding and integrating assets. Individual aircrew technique must also be nothing short of excellent. Beyond the academics of SLATS that Strike provides, air wing training is the practice.

Integration of every aspect of wing work tends to be emphasized over unit-level training (available to units at home or on the boat), because integration of all available assets has become the real world of strike warfare (see Strike DET Syllabus).

But Strike also realizes that each wing is at a different stage in its typical turnaround training

Crew uses power loader to hoist 1,000-pound "Walleye" smart bomb onto A-7 wing pylon.

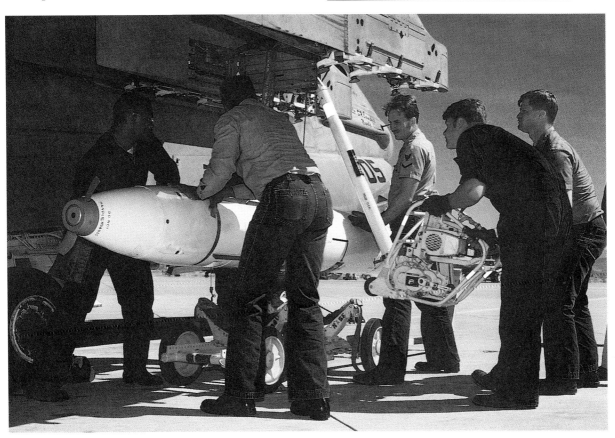

Strike skipper ''Bubba'' Brodsky ripple-fires octet of 5-inch Zuni rockets over Bravo-17 range.

cycle after it is reformed, and that individual crews are at different experience levels, so time is allotted for individual squadron training work in the overall schedule worked out between the CAG and the Strike planning staff (see sample DET activities on Strike DET Syllabus).

UNIT-LEVEL TRAINING

Typical DETs start low key, with first work designed to clear the cobwebs of recent routine squadron work and get aircrews up to speed on all the locale's advantages and opportunities.

Initial Fallon-area ''fam'' (familiarization) is followed by section and division tactics, including weapons delivery, ACM (including dissimilar aircraft, such as Aggressors), and attention-getting day/night low-level work over mountainous terrain, with which the Fallon area is richly endowed. Because so much of the Fallon range effort is dedicated to creating complete EW/IADS threat environments, time is spent on EW work and checking out the aircraft electronic systems.

STRIKE DET SYLLABUS: OVERVIEW

Formal air wing training is typically divided into six phases and three ancillary programs. Air wing deployment schedules are based on an eighteen-day DET. A generic schedule (each wing has its own) might be:

Phases	Day	Schedule
• Unit-level training	1	Fly-in/ground training
• Close air support (CAS)	2–3	Unit-level/ground training TAC/RECCE
• Overland air superiority training (OAST)	4–6	CAS/TAC RECCE
• Fleet-integrated suppression training (FIST)	7	No fly
• Strike phase	8–11	OAST/CSAR
• Advanced training phase (ATP)	12–13	FIST/strikes/CSAR
	14	No fly
Programs	16–18	Advanced training phase
• Air wing intelligence training	18	Debrief/fly-off
• TAC RECCE training		
• Combat SAR training		

Each CAG uses this ''menu'' to plan and schedule his wing's training program to meet its precise needs.

INTELLIGENCE

Intel training was incorporated into the air wing training program to augment SLATS and to correct operational shortfalls ranging from an overall lack of strike-planner awareness of available intelligence assets to intel community failure to tailor intel support adequately for strike planning.

The intel work is usually done in two phases during the DET's first week. The first phase is a series of briefs from Strike's intel department, covering Fallon-area intelligence concepts, tactical intel, collection methods, electronic warfare integration, and cryptology. The second phase is a strike-planning seminar designed as two-way discussion on how to apply tactical intelligence concepts to real-world scenarios.

What are the intel sources? Strike is particularly reticent in discussing the intel area, but many of the sources are known: long- and short-term geopolitical situation data, current military activity and overall capabilities (men, weapons, and deployment), target data of all kinds, and data passed on from local sources.

Another major battle group intelligence source is TARPS (Tactical Air Reconnaissance Pod System), and a training program for TARPS squadrons is taught by Strike as a special subject. Whatever the external difficulties, TARPS is one facet of intelligence gathering that is under air wing control!

TARPS

Tactical reconnaissance training at Strike provides realistic, overland work both for aircrew and wing intelligence specialists. Why the emphasis? Because fleet overland TARPS training, using the TARPS pod on one of the F-14's Phoenix stations, tends to be limited to relatively benign low-level routes ("No low-level work is truly benign," comes the reminder from Comdr. Jon Green, recent skipper of Lemoore's Hornet reserve squadron, VFA-303) that squadron pilots end up learning "like a commute drive." This can lead to tactical deficiencies when TARPS sorties must cover targets in hostile environments. Wings are well aware that TARPS is one of their most valuable data sources on targets.

A related problem of repeatedly flying known routes to known targets, for practice, is photointerpretation of land targets by intelligence specialists (IS) assigned to TARPS-equipped F-14 squadrons. Familiarity breeds laziness. Every time a wing comes to Fallon, it faces what is, in effect, an entirely new range—in the eighteen months between visits, the Fallon range areas develop rapidly and visibly.

Two-phase TARPS training—twelve day and twelve night sorties—normally comes early in the DET, with all routes, scenarios, and targets provided and coordinated by NSWC.

—TARPS PHOTOINTERPRETATION

To hone the intelligence specialists' land-target identification skills, two local IFR (instrument flight rule) sorties are flown (two day, two night) over routes chosen for IS training in support of air intelligence officer training. These sorties give aircrews a chance to train in low-level nav and target acquisition over unfamiliar terrain—always a challenge and an essential task for aircrew.

Eight TARPS sorties are flown on TACTS using the Echo Whiskey and Bravo 17 ranges,

EW because of the wide range of electronic threats, and B-17 because of its multifaceted target areas. These TARPS sweeps challenge aircrew ability to photograph military and industrial targets in hostile environments.

What does the air wing skipper look for in his TARPS pilots as the result of these TACTS sorties? He expects to see improved ingress skills (including effective use of terrain), better evasive behavior in the target area—while also obtaining the photos, of course!—and egress tactics that optimize survival. For these evolutions, Strike

will provide scenarios before the squadron DET to Fallon to allow the squadron to convene its TARPS mission-planning board if it wants. Almost all take advantage of this opportunity.

COMBAT SEARCH AND RESCUE (CSAR)

Navy aircraft and crew losses during attempted rescues in Vietnam were shocking, unacceptable. How bad was the problem? One aircraft was

lost in every four rescue attempts, and one aircrew member every eight attempts. That's how bad.

To reverse that sad and unacceptable situation, the Navy has made CSAR training integral to the wing turnaround training cycle, further reinforced during the Strike DET at Fallon each air wing includes in that cycle.

Strike has worked up a ten-event program, working with various outside groups. Those groups include the SEALs (Sea, Air, Land)—SEAL Team One, in Coronado, near San Diego, supplies an officer on the Strike staff to whom,

as with all the crazed SEALs, red meat must be thrown daily.

SEALs are a Navy activity, little known and even less understood outside the activity itself, that undertakes some of the most difficult, dangerous, and physically arduous activities in naval

---

Opposite page: Smoked F-14 crew uses signal mirror and hand-held emergency radio to call in rescue helo. *Below:* We're outa here! Lifesaving SH-3 helo alights for mere seconds as downed crew piles in for rescue.

War paint: SEAL recon duo uses laser designator to "paint" ground target for smart-ordnance-equipped strike aircraft.

warfare. These tasks include what used to be known as UDT (underwater demolition team) work of clearing planned landing beaches of mines or obstructions, being dropped offshore by parachute carrying scuba gear to dive and swim to targets for various tasks (e.g., laser target designation where targets are small or hard to see from the air), and for the vital activity of retrieving aircrew downed in hostile territory—CSAR.

Also included is HC-9, a reserve helo squadron based at North Island, San Diego, the only squadron in the Navy dedicated full time to CSAR work. HC-9 provides its helicopter assets and CSAR aircrew training, and Strike encourages wings to bring assigned HS squadrons if they can (the trip is arduous for East Coast helo squadrons, at 100 knots cruise, but at least selected crews can participate, sharing HC-9 assets).

All wing aircrew get CSAR training, to learn about isolated personnel reports (also called ISO-PREPS), guidelines on evasion, intelligence, evasive plans of action, and the codes used by CSAR teams as unequivocal identification of downed aircrew based on personal data that escalate from the general to the specific, to provide unequivocal ID and eliminate the possibility of enemy traps under the guise of a downed aircrew member.

Then pilots and crews "killed" in earlier missions are taken out into the hostile Nevada environment to see how well the lessons have been learned. Both day and night CSAR evolutions are run, ending up with helo and SEAL rescues (called, in official jargon, "extraction methods").

CLOSE AIR SUPPORT

"Close air support is integral to Navy/Marine amphibious operations," explains Pat Doyle. "Recent Grenada experience taught the Navy, once again, that all facets of close air support must be exercised thoroughly and regularly. Strike's CAS program is procedure oriented, to standardize, to make sure wings are current in CAS doctrine and real-world C^2 [command-and-control] procedures."

CAS is a two- to four-day evolution with both preplanned and FAC-briefed day and night missions. The C^2 structure and types of target marking match current amphibious-operations doctrine. Mortar teams, AAA units, and ground forward air controllers are prepositioned on the range.

"In addition to Marine FACs, Strike also provides training opportunities for Army, Navy, and Air Force personnel in FAC procedures, both air and ground," explains Doyle. "At times each branch has provided CAS target control in a single day."

CAS sorties normally consist of a section of aircraft executing a preplanned mission and two to four ad hoc ones. The section is typically routed through various contact and IP (initial point) locations to provide nav and timing training—it's vital to hit TOT (time over target) on the nose for truly effective missions. FACs mark targets with Willie Pete (white phosphorus) mortar or artillery rounds. Other methods include marking the target with a laser spot or a radar beacon placed on the target itself.

Want more realism? Strike provides it. "Smokey SAMs"—small, styrofoam, expendable rockets with fins—erupt from the range into the path of incoming attackers, trailing smoke that makes them look close enough to the real thing that they bring back adrenalin-charged memories for crew with Vietnam, Lebanon, or Libya experience.

How did we do? Fair question. Daylight CAS missions are videotaped from the ground FAC site. Tapes are provided to aircrew the same day, often in association with TACTS debriefs, to let aircrew study their technique—ingress, weapons delivery, egress—from the perspective of an enemy SAM/AAA site operator.

OVERLAND AIR SUPERIORITY TRAINING

OAST (Overland Air Superiority Training)

was designed by Strike in collaboration with Top Gun, initially for fighter-tactics training. It has evolved. Now it highlights long-needed tactical dialogue and increased awareness of mission needs between attack, fighter, and AEW (airborne early-warning) groups as vital elements of air wing mission integration.

Integrating the core of a wing's strike force is the OAST prime directive: an attack element dedicated to destroying a target, a fighter element dedicated to strike support by protecting that attack element, and the E-2C tasked with C^2.

OAST runs four days with daily morning and afternoon events. Each tactical problem is "time compressed" (under fifteen minutes) to allow two runs per event. Each event normally involves six attack, four to six fighter, and one AEW aircraft, but all other elements that would normally be involved in a strike are considered in the scenario presentation. Threats are tailored to meet specific building-block objectives. Adversary aircraft assigned to oppose the missions meld their tactics to ensure the desired scenario presentations.

Strike is nothing if not thorough, and this is the kind of attention to detail that makes the difference of many hours of effort on the part of the hard-pressed visiting wing: charts, kneeboard cards, overheads, and so forth are prepared in advance on the TAMPS computer for use by strike leaders. Each event has a target, strike

TA-7 rolls into the weeds for eye-opening low-level run-in.

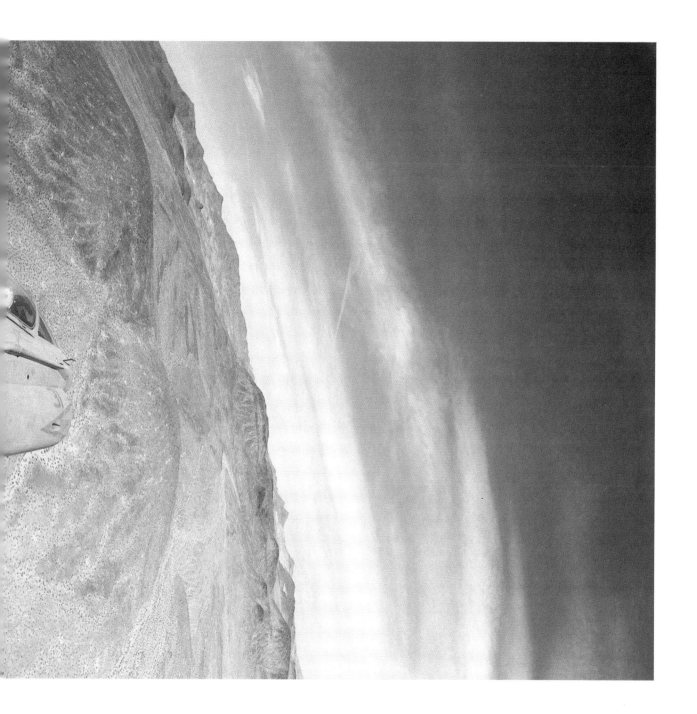

weaponeering fighter mission, and strike ingress route. Neat.

"OAST is a learning environment," says Pat. "There have been many superb training objectives introduced during the program's development. It's not a 'test' of a wing's capabilities; it's concentrated, graduate-level training in integrated strike-warfare tactics."

FLEET INTEGRATED SUPPRESSION TRAINING (FIST)

"Defense suppression is critical in strike planning. With increasing threat density and sophistication (in the latest IADS environments), strike assets *will not survive unless enemy air defenses are suppressed*," asserts Doyle (emphasis added).

Party line? Hardly. The message is devastatingly direct. Immortality is not conferred on attack aircraft in the days of the modern IADS. It's not a matter of luck, if it ever was.

FIST was started in mid-1987 to provide continuity between OAST and the strike phase. It was conceived to rectify deficiencies during the strike and advanced training phases.

FIST is targeted for strike/division leaders, ARM (antiradiation missile) shooters, decoys, and E-2C as well as EA-6B aircrews. As with OAST, NSWC recommends diverse wing participation. Two or three days are dedicated to FIST, with a day and a night event scheduled daily. As with OAST, the tactical problem in the first four events is time compressed to get two runs per event. The fifth event is exercised only once.

Aircraft vary with event—normally one or two EA-6Bs, an E-2C, two to four fighters, two to four ARM launchers, one or two ALDV (air-launched drone vehicle) launchers, and two to four strike aircraft. Following the OAST example, each event stands alone, tailored for building-block goals. Much of the admin work is already done—data such as knee-board cards, charts, and so on are preprepped on TAMPS.

"Target destruction and force survival are the ultimate goals of defense suppression," Pat says by way of emphasis. "FIST provides the air wing with the strategies and integration training to achieve these goals."

STRIKE PHASE

After OAST and FIST, the air group commander assembles his assets to plan and execute coordinated/integrated "stand-alone" strikes. Normally a maximum of three strikes per day (two day, one night) are flown. Exceeding this rate degrades detailed planning/execution, prevents strike leaders from physically obtaining essential assets, and forces them to use "constructive" elements (thus defeating the concept of "integrated" air wing training). In addition, trying to do too much burns out the wing just before the advanced training phase.

NSWC suggests that CAGs utilize a mix of local and out-of-area (Nellis/Utah Test Range/ Saylor Creek/China Lake) targets. The trade-off: thorough debriefs are available at Fallon's TACTS facilities, but valuable training comes with the task of navigating to, acquiring, and striking unfamiliar targets.

Strike assigns a representative to help each strike leader. For work outside the Fallon complex, NSWC's out-of-area target coordinator provides strike leaders with a single point of contact, responsible for prefiled routes to and from the various targets, and ATC (air traffic control) airspace liaison (the Federal Aviation Agency has controllers on duty at Fallon to help coordinate traffic).

Even in the West—CAVU with big skies and light traffic—such coordination is vital. It's quite typical of Strike's attention to detail that this sort of local help would be made available.

ADVANCED TRAINING PHASE (ATP)

"The ATP is the culmination of a wing's Fallon DET," says Brodsky. In the ATP, the integrated tactical training of the previous phases is exercised in a three-day campaign battle problem. Once again, it is not scored, because it is not a graded test of a wing's ability to conduct strike warfare but an advanced *training* evolution.

An "in-brief" (a lecture presentation given to participants to introduce administrative requirements and training objectives before the evolution itself) is given forty-eight hours before the first strike and provides the over-all target scenario, order of battle, and associated data. In 1988, the scenario was an inland target complex in Bravo 17, and the order of battle a modern IADS (a system controlled by modern computers) manned by experienced and capable operators (Strike staff!).

Real-time intel plays a vital role in this phase, which is the reason why the battle problem was expanded to three days with not more than two strikes per day. This allows, as Pat Doyle explains it, "realistic intelligence feedback to strike planners on the success of their previous strikes."

Unlike other scenarios, in which "kills" can "come back to life," attrition in the ATP is cumulative both for aircraft and weapons (but *not* for aircrew, to whom the training is vital), so CAG must consider asset conservation as his strike evolution unfolds. All ATP strikes are conducted on TACTS to help reconstruct the events and debrief in detail. This makes for maximum nakedness on the part of aircrew as they look at what happened and what might have been.

51

TACTS, TAMPS, and TEAMS

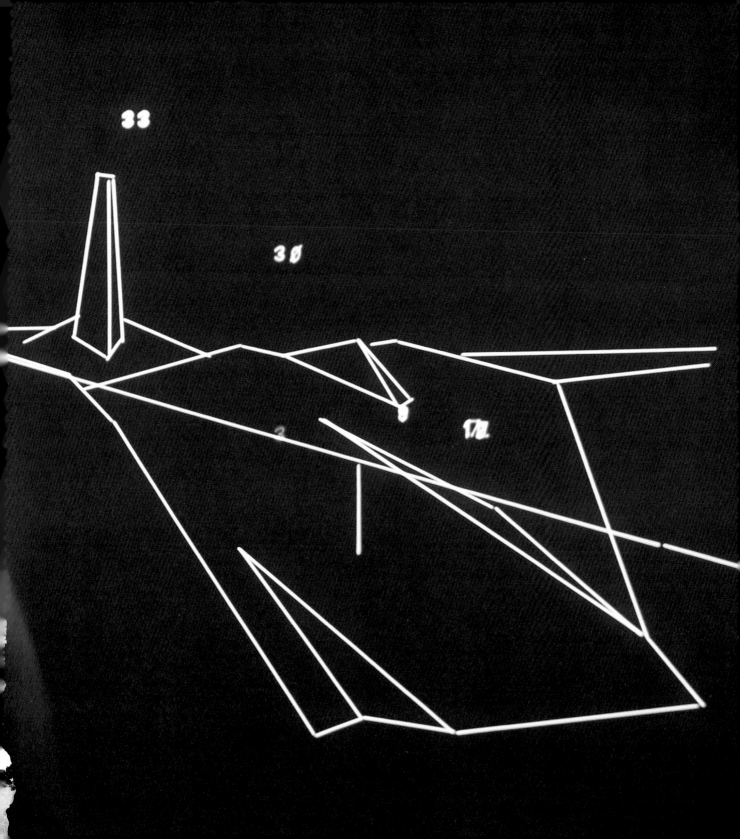

TACTS. Tactical Air Combat Training System. TACTS—five little letters that have come to mean a great deal in the air wings. They mean just as much to aircrew who come to Fallon for Strike training: to fly and fight, to suffer and learn. TACTS stands for a lot of technology and a huge investment by the Navy. But the system started humbly, under a different acronym. It has evolved dramatically. TAMPS (Tactical Aircraft Mission Planning System) and TEAMS (Tactical Electronic [Warfare] Aircraft Mission Support) are the two other major computer systems that have brought great leaps forward in effective training at Strike and around the fleet.

ACMR TECHNOLOGY

TACTS had its beginnings as ACMR (air-combat maneuvering range) back in the late sixties and early seventies. Cubic Corporation of San Diego first developed the electronic system for tracking virtually any type of combat aircraft in real time through on-board sensors, microwave telemetry, and computer-driven ground displays.

The very first Navy/Marine Corps ACMR system was introduced at MCAS Yuma (where many individual members of the Desert Mafia flew) in the early 1970s, installed with its offices and major equipment in a set of crude and distinctly temporary-looking trailers. Temporary? Hardly. But back then, it was, like so many new technology ideas, an unproved concept.

The new and highly developed TACTS system is based on continuous refinement of the original system concept based on the advances that have occurred in computing and microwave technologies. Tracking high-speed aircraft in real time doesn't begin to tell the full technical story. ACMR—or TACTS, as the Navy now calls it—comprises four essential elements, or subsystems, known as AIS (Airborne Instrumentation Subsystem), TIS (Tracking Instrumentation Subsystem), CCS (Control and Communications Subsystem), and DDS (Display and Debrief Subsystem).

In part the system is what you see on the wingtip of your F-14 or F/A-18, your A-6 or A-7—indeed, virtually any of the current fighter, attack, and support aircraft in the allied inventories—an orange, wingless pod very close to the size and shape of a Sidewinder, bolted onto your airplane on any Aero-38, LAU-7A, or 16S200 hard-point or launcher rack. Time to attach: two minutes!

The AIS can monitor virtually all the key behaviors of your aircraft, this very instant—airspeed, attitude, angle of attack, altitude, simulated weapon status—and transmit all this information to the ground in real time (instantaneously) via microwave telemetry.

The system is also in part a set of microwave

Check six! TACTS simulator reproduces Tomcat back-seater's view between twin tails.

Cubic TACTS data-transmission pods, painted orange, are uploaded for strike mission (one per aircraft).

telemetry receivers sited on convenient nearby mountaintops, on the ranges below, that receive information from the pods on the airplanes. This is the TIS.

The CCS passes airborne data to a set of massive, full-color displays back in the debrief area. They are driven by computers that tell you, and a room full of your peers, for the record, like it or not, what you did and how well (or badly) you did it.

The last part of the TACTS, the DDS, also allows all air-to-air and air-to-ground communi-cations to be similarly monitored and played back . . . for the record.

The software working inside the bank of four Perkin-Elmer TACTS computers is not trivial, and, beyond unmeasurable instrumentation varia-tions that the experts say are irrelevant, and no matter what aircrew may claim, TACTS does

TACTS pod transmits real-time flight data during A-6 bombing hop.

not lie. It has, well, no tact, a fact to which Strike visitors will attest grudgingly. It is the final and soulless electronic arbiter of a pilot's approach to a problem evolution, and it reveals for the record if he has accomplished a kill or has himself been smoked. They keep archival tapes . . . for the record.

Cubic's first ACMR system could initially handle four aircraft in all—the fight being monitored and recorded could involve 1-v-1, -2, or -3 or 2-v-2. That was it. It was more than enough—it was devastating to ACM participants. Then, in the early seventies, it was an electronic marvel, and the gouge went out quickly to fleet pilots and crew by the usual jungle telegraph as if ACMR were some kind of magic. In a way, that's just what it was. As it has developed and improved, it has become even more magical. And there is even more magic up the sleeves of the clever engineers at Cubic.

The meaning of ACMR was plain for all to see, then as now. Its punch was telegraphed by a sign outside the entrance to the Yuma trailers that spelled an end to the endless bar-call braggadocio that is—or at least used to be, before ACMR came along to shut him up—your average loud-mouthed fighter or attack pilot's lifeblood: "The bullshit stops here."

True. It pitched ACM headlong into the computer age, an era of shooting safe, economical, and reusable electrons of all shapes and sizes, not costly bullets, bombs, or missiles. And . . . it worked.

EVOLUTION INTO TACTS

Today TACTS stands for Tactical Air Combat Training System, reflecting the fact that ACM—no matter what the Top Gun folks claim—is only one part of a greatly expanded operational capability. Nowhere is this more important than at Strike. The Navy's biggest and most advanced TACTS is at Fallon.

At Fallon, dirt matters—even Nevada dirt. The ground range elements (see Chapter One) are as or more important than what goes on in the air, plane to plane. Because Fallon and Strike are not just about the glamorous business of monitoring fighters going at it eye to eye and hand to hand.

At Fallon, it is not just ACM that counts. The place and the training are much broader in scope, all about the essential strike activities of moving dirt, of inflicting pain on targets down there, of understanding and analyzing electronic and surface-to-air threats.

That's at the "front end." That's the mission, the evolution. TACTS shows you what happened next—what you decided to do about it all, and how well you met your plan, whether you took the right action to neutralize all those threats, the degree to which you comprehended and acted upon the overall power and danger of the fully equipped and capably operated modern IADS that U.S. and allied pilots are finding in place worldwide.

And, in addition, there was still the air threat to consider and counter.

In the case of Fallon's TACTS range, the system can also show—with a few limitations that are going away one by one—what the IADS guys on the ground are doing to make life miserable for the attack group. To see it is an education. John Lehman didn't insist on calling it Strike U. for nothing, even though it's "Strike" to the staff. Learn . . . and live.

Entire air wing sits in on daily mission briefing. CAG-9, Capt. Bob Canepa, is front and center in khakis.

The first ACMR system was designed and used exclusively for air-(to-air) combat maneuvering, or ACM, the stiffly formal descriptors for the manic world of dogfighting. It covered select range geography in the Yuma vicinity. They named the ranges then, including one operating area whimsically called "Rakish Litter." That first, embryonic system showed the ground on the displays—terrain masking was one of the tactics that could be monitored and evaluated, and the hills and mountains were incorporated into the display. But the ability of the system to replicate serious ground threats was minimal.

Rakish Litter. Hmmm—not a bad name. The litter is real: the detritus of air-to-ground bombing. And it is rakish by any definition—unexploded Mark 82 leftovers, 20 Mike Mike casings scattered around the surplus tanks, and APCs and buses and half-tracks trucked in from military

All Fallon range activity is controlled from this position in the basement of radar tower on the base (*right*).

dumps around the West to be used as targets. Then there are the occasional skeletons of a combat aircraft or ten, such as F-4Bs and F-4Ns that had experienced annoying little BLC (boundary layer control) fires, A-4s and A-7s that quit without a way to get them home (memo to self, but no time to commit it to writing: "time to step outside"); or the distractions of the occasional midair during ACM, which can really ruin your day.

Today there are TACTS systems not just at Yuma and Fallon but at many Navy and Air Force sites around the world, including TAC's sprawling Nellis AFB; the Navy's East Coast Top Gun clone at NAS Oceana, near Norfolk, Virginia; Clark AFB in the Philippines; and RAF Alconbury in England, from which the USAFE

Tactical Air Command aircraft fly. The Air Force calls its systems ACMI (air-combat maneuvering instrumentation). The systems are designed to be fully compatible, so that aircraft from Nellis or Yuma will work on Fallon's TACTS system if they enter the area, as they so often do.

NATO also has an ACMI system in place on and near the Mediterranean island of Sardinia, west of Italy, on which U.S., British, and other NATO aircraft fly regularly, using (among other features) buoys instead of mountaintop relays. For extra efficiency, solar, wind, or thermal electric generator equipment supplies power to remote Tracking Instrumentation Subsystem elements.

FALLON'S TACTS

Fallon's "new, improved" TACTS attained IOC (initial operational capability) in spring 1985, and after the usual period of teething and troubleshooting it is now fully operational at very high levels of reliability. And performance—nothing short of spectacular!

New Cubic systems of the late eighties, such as those at Fallon, can handle up to thirty-six aircraft instead of the original four. In addition to monitoring signal outputs from these thirty-six aircraft, Fallon's TACTS system can also maintain "position-only" data on twenty-four pod-equipped aircraft. That's a grand total of sixty—virtually a complete, coordinated air wing evolution! In training, in practice, this full sixty-aircraft capacity is seldom reached.

Electronic and physical threats can be simulated from the ground, as well, that will show incoming strike groups a broad range of known and anticipated bad stuff that may come from the typical IADS down on the ground. Furthermore, ordnance drops can now be scored electronically, based on aircraft dynamics—attitude, airspeed, and heading versus the ground—at the instant the weapon is "pickled." This is NDBS (no-drop bomb scoring) for attacking point targets even if identified only by map reference or called by a ground or air FAC (forward air controller), who may also drop smoke markers. Not to be chauvinistic about such matters, Strike uses Army FACs as well as Navy and Marine units. Many of these features are unique to Fallon, but will inevitably spread to other systems around the world.

TACTS is many things to Strike and to the wings. It's an electronic scorekeeper and umpire; it's an educational tool and training aid; it's invaluable in analyzing the effectiveness and use of intelligence.

Up to seventeen real and thirteen simulated EW threats (AAA or SAM tracking radars, for example) can be presented and processed, which gives TACTS the capability of presenting the appearance of a full IADS environment to aircrew in a wide variety of scenarios from simple to complex. A library of "doctrinal" behaviors of essentially any potential adversary throughout the world is available for presentation to strike groups. As many as fifty weapons events, singly or (much more likely) in combinations, can be handled concurrently in the TACTS by the hard-worked Strike operations staff, including both simulated ordnance that would be carried on a typical training exercise as well as typical air-to-air and surface-to-air threats.

In addition to the established AIM-7 Sparrow and AIM-9 Sidewinder, as carried by "Blue"

CAP (combat air-patrol) aircraft flown by the wings, the system can also simulate Soviet AAMs (air-to-air missiles), as carried by "Red" Aggressor aircraft, as well as the Soviet SA-2, -3, -6 and -8 SAMs and ZSU-23/4 AAA ground threats. Eventually the system may enable the pilot to see and hear the threat in the cockpit (it would illuminate the radar warning system with the appropriate signal) and would show up in the system, on the screen, just as if the real thing were on the air electronically and in the air physically, but this capability is not yet in place.

In the air-to-ground mode, simulations can be made within TACTS of antiradiation ordnance, such as the AGM-45A Shrike and, in the future, the AGM-88 HARM (high-speed antiradiation missile); conventional high-drag weaponry, such as the antipersonnel Mark 82 Snakeye with its massive deployable tailfins that increase

Ground threat radar on range gives attacking pilots ultra-realistic simulation of SAM/AAA unpleasantness.

drag; and antiarmor or antipersonnel nastiness, typified by the Mark 20 Rockeye and CBU-59 and the Mark 76/106 practice bombs.

NDBS (no-drop bomb scoring) for air-to-ground bomb simulation is matched by the NLMS, or no-launch missile scoring, used for AAM/AIM (air-intercept missile) ACM training.

A VIEW TO A KILL

As perhaps the biggest and best electronic

Dave "Deach" di Chiara, himself a recon RF-4C Phantom backseater with the Nevada Air National Guard, manages TACTS control console as part of Fallon civilian contract team.

training system ever created, the real TACTS action for everyone but the pilots and ground operating staff involved is in the DDS (Display and Debrief Subsystem). Curiously, many civilian viewers of the movie *Top Gun* were boggled most by the TACTS display system and regarded it as the least-likely piece of technology seen

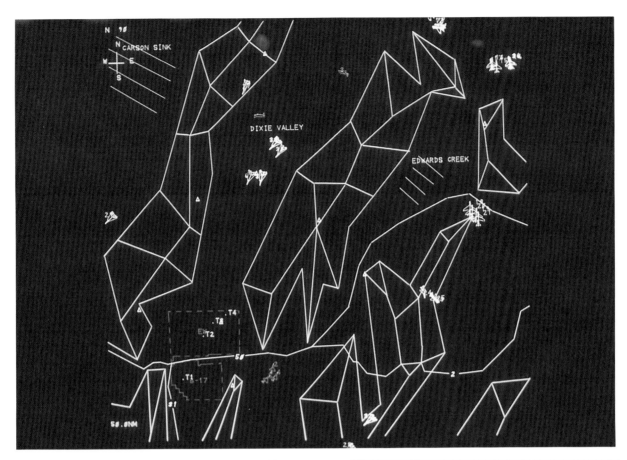

on the movie screen. In fact, it was the film's most authentic action!

As currently configured at Fallon, the DDS comprises operator consoles at which tasks are monitored and the large-scale, full-color display screens used for mass debriefs. In addition to Strike staff who conduct the training work, daily system operation and maintenance are handled by an outside contractor.

Everything can be shown, either in graphic or alphanumeric form, with all the aircraft in an exercise color coded as to ''Red'' (adversary),

''God's-eye'' TACTS view of Fallon ranges. Tomcat CAP sweep is at center; attackers are terrain-masking at top and center right. Note Aggressor gaggle (red planes) lying in wait by target at bottom!

''Blue'' (friendly), or other activity. Scales can range from close in, a ''microscopic view'' as little as one mile on the screen axes in which individual aircraft can easily be identified by type, to a ''macro'' of entire ranges covering tens of miles or more (there is a point at which useful detail is lost).

There's nowhere to hide. The view can be rotated 360 degrees in azimuth and the full 90 degrees from directly above ("God's eye") to the horizon, with all the terrain features moving (terrain masking by aircraft can be seen as clearly as or better than by the unaided or binoculared eye in the real world). No clouds obscure the vision, for example. The red faces at debriefs speak volumes.

Weapons tracks after release are presented in flight as dashed lines that show precise trajectory. When scored, an ACM "kill" also causes a coffin, whose symbolism is obvious, to be drawn around the aircraft destroyed.

There's more. In real time, or later for review, the screens show a pilot's-eye view of the action, forward from the cockpit or even rotated to his "six," with all aircraft dynamics displayed in alphanumerics, so that information as detailed as individual aircraft energy states can be monitored from second to second.

Navy appreciation of TACTS is not in doubt, and the results delivered by the system in training at Strike prove it. In the Fall 1987 issue of *Tail Hook,* a much-read magazine in naval-aviation circles, Bubba Brodsky heaps praise on TACTS in a major Strike feature article: "The beauty [of the TACTS system] is that we now have detailed accountability in the attack community. The TACTS monitor on the range is the key. With 36 airplanes carefully tracked, the attack pilot can no longer make mistakes without everyone knowing.

Neither can the fighter escort 'arc off' after attacking bogeys, leaving the strike aircraft vulnerable. Even little things such as a sloppy pulloff at the wrong altitude cannot go unnoticed.

While all of this activity is going on, the strike group has to deal with 20 simulated threats on the EW range before the aircraft gets to the target. The results are immediate and honest: we know who got shot down—and why—and we can discuss it with aircrew as soon as they get out of the airplane.

Is there any way to beat the system? Experienced attack and fighter pilots who have flown TACTS a lot have in some cases learned to try. Human nature. One example, being rectified, is the way a strike group can approach the range from an area where system coverage is not yet implemented.

Sometimes wings try to beat the system by bending the rules. One of the ROE (rules-of-engagement) criteria, for example, is that the wing E-2C may not monitor the TACTS control frequency that operates as GCI (ground-controlled intercept) for "Red" fighters going for an interception. On one occasion, the Strike TACTS staff, knowing that its comm was being monitored, got sweet revenge on one such wise guy by calling in a bunch of imaginary fighters ("Oh, my God," said the E-2 CICO, "where are those goddamned fighters? I can't see them on my scope!"). Gotcha!

FUTURE TACTS

Where will TACTS go from here? The Navy and Cubic are understandably closemouthed about it, but some obvious development paths can be discerned: extend the geographical reach of the system, improve ground-target density and detail, increase the number of airplanes it can handle, fill the threat gaps the system cannot yet simulate, and maintain its overall capability

EA-6B backseat wizards Lt. Steve "Kirbs" Kirby and Capt. John "Action" Blum, USMC, prep their ECM mission on TEAMS computer system.

versus the moving targets of IADS.

Another area that seems likely to see attention in future is the increasing use of RPVs (remotely piloted vehicles) as adjuncts to existing systems. For example, Grumman has proposed an unmanned complement to the E-2C in the form of a VSTOL (very short take-off and landing) RPV that can operate for up to fourteen hours at altitudes over 30,000 feet for over-the-horizon sensor extension, and the proposed vehicle has been shown to be launchable and recoverable from a destroyer

in severe weather. Details on this system were revealed to the public in unclassified reports carried in *Aviation Week* ("Aviation Leak," say its critics) and in *Defense Electronics*. Note, too, that Strike hosted a classified Navy/civilian RPV summit meeting in late 1987, reflecting escalated interest in these potentially powerful pieces of technology.

Technologically, TACTS developments abound. Fifth-generation computing capabilities, expanded data storage, "expert" artificial-intelligence developments, and larger screens with more detail all the way to holographic (three-dimensional) display techniques when they become commercially available can also realistically be anticipated as DARPA (Defense Advanced Research Projects Agency) and the Navy move ahead on development. Fallon, possessing the largest and most elaborate TACTS in service, is almost certainly the first place such next-generation equipment would be installed and tried before full IOC (initial operational capability) around the world.

Beyond existing systems noted earlier, TACTS systems are being implemented at key locales worldwide. These include a system for

PK (probability of kill) prognosis: brightest colors show greatest threat intensity on TAMPS target simulator. Ideal ingress/lob/egress path is shown by white track at top left.

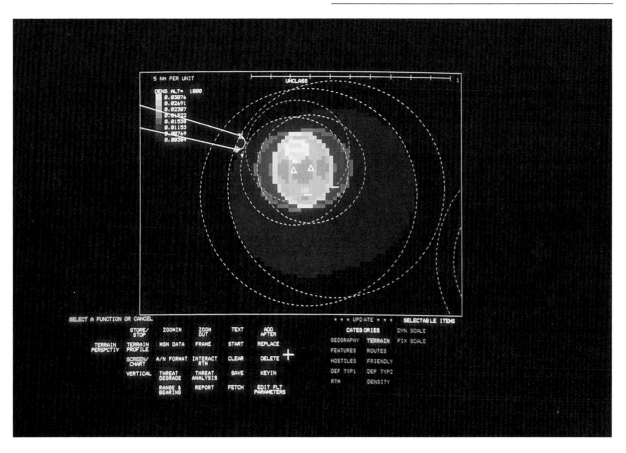

the Royal Canadian Air Force at Goose Bay, Labrador. Thailand, already modernizing its IADS, has bought a TACTS. NATO has been considering expansion from its single site in Sardinia to a range at Konya, in Turkey, and other sites, including Portugal, have been reviewed.

Aircraft from other nations, including the British Buccaneers and Anglo-French Jaguars, have already flown TACTS/ACMI ranges, especially at Nellis in Red Flag. The recent visit of West German Panavia Tornados to Fallon is not coincidence, even though no joint U.S.-allied exercises

have yet been flown there.

Carrier-based TACTS is another future use being talked about, at least conceptually. Such a system would enable Strike-type training, as well as ACM work, to be undertaken repeatedly even during blue-water operations. And blue-water ACM or strikes on seagoing targets are obviously an integral part of a wing's overall task.

TAMPS terrain: sortie track (white) indicates optimum route, best terrain masking.

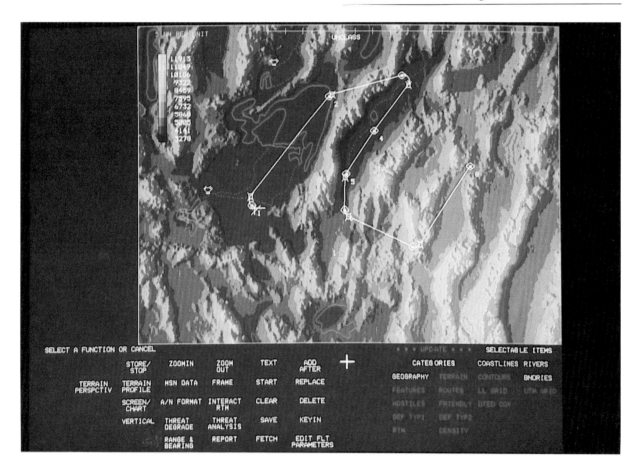

Typical problem-solution scenarios will then clearly have to include submarine threats and ASW responses.

But TACTS alone is not the whole story. The Strike capability owes much to its TAMPS and TEAMS systems. Although much smaller and lower in cost, both systems deliver tremendous training value.

TAMPS

"Instant" mission planning. Sure—why not? With new computer technology almost anything is possible. TAMPS (Tactical Aircraft Mission Planning System) from McDonnell Douglas has become a Fleet "standard operating procedure" (SOP), and technological SOPs must prove their value beyond doubt before they are accepted by the working folks. The system is now aboard every boat and all Tomahawk-shooting fleet ships, as well as at Strike.

TAMPS's computer, based on a DEC Micro-VAX processor, literally automates mission planning. Using the system, a strike planner and mission leader can create in a matter of minutes a detailed mission plan that would otherwise take hours. So sophisticated is the system that it lets the user model a virtually unlimited number of alternative plans versus threats, terrain, and other considerations and scores the options as to probability of success. Tomahawk missions can be integrated in the system, just as they can be in a strike.

TAMPS can even accommodate the kind of significant but overlooked detail that no ordinary mortal—especially not a mission leader or planner with hundreds of pressing priorities—could possibly take time to consider. Would you believe accurate prediction of incident light, including moonlight, corrected for phase of the moon, terrain-shadow effects, and time to the fraction of a second that would permit (or deny) use of night-vision goggles at any geographic spot on earth? Yup.

Some system, TAMPS. The system library includes an up-to-date inventory of all the electronic and associated physical threats (AAA, SAM) in every world locale of interest to the Navy, updated "often" (don't ask) by the various intel assets available to the Department of Defense (DoD) (don't ask). Threats are displayed in terms of location, type, and observation/physical "reach." After a planner has modeled his intended ingress/pop-up/egress route versus those threats, the system scores him on the probability of mission success.

Terrain models in system memory come from the global digital maps, based on a one-meter grid, generated from satellite observations and stored originally by the Defense Mapping Agency (DMA), which serves the DoD. So? So the mission planner can plot a route and way points, see where he can hide through terrain masking, when he will be vulnerable to illumination from the threats, when he can jam with his Prowler.

Terrain views can be displayed in essentially any form, at any angle from ground level to directly above, and can even be presented color authentic in terms of incident-sun illumination based on time of day. Future developments will enable a strike planner to "prefly" an entire mission in the system.

The system knows the envelope of every fleet aircraft in its library, as well as Tomahawk performance profiles, and can calculate virtually every useful aspect of aircraft behavior on a mission. For example, it can calculate (and print out for a knee board) fuel used between way points and remaining on return, based on latitude and longitude, altitude, airspeed, and ordnance load, including "fudge" factors for an aggressive pilot or for a wingie who must juggle throttle setting to keep up with his lead and the actual, real-world aerodynamics of a working fleet bird. Remember, those performance figures were taken on new, clean airplanes that had never seen the realities of fleet use.

Outputs from TAMPS are vital at Strike. Kneeboard printouts are only one example of TAMPS's prodigious powers. All mission data are interdependent, so the system works as a kind of "spread sheet" in which any alteration is reflected instantly in all the other numbers and in any printout.

TEAMS

Some of the most challenging work done in the Strike world surrounds electronic warfare, or EW. Mission planning that focuses on this complex problem area is done with TEAMS (Tactical Electronic [Warfare] Aircraft Mission Support), from the fertile minds of PRB (the appropriately named "Pax River Boys"), retired aviators who came mostly from NAS Patuxent River and from the Prowler community, whose offices and plant are now located close to the Navy's famed test-pilot activity at Patuxent River in Maryland.

Based on a Texas Instruments 990 microprocessor, the TEAMS system (a dyadic, or "double," system on each boat and at Whidbey), is, in effect, a specialized subset of TAMPS. But the problems are so intricate—threat radar frequency and other characteristics, HARM launch criteria, jammer options and abilities, to name only three mission facets—that a separate system is needed for planning.

Perhaps the most interesting output of either TEAMS or TAMPS is the four-track, 1.6-megabyte tape cassette TEAMS delivers once a mission has been planned. It is taken to the Prowler, and its contents are loaded into the EW system, thus "installing" a complete set of mission details (which can be manually changed or overridden in flight, of course). Better yet, a matching cartridge system on the airplane records all the actual mission activity so that detailed debriefs are quick and easy.

TACTS, TAMPS, and TEAMS. A terrific trio of technological tricks making a big difference in the quality of training at Strike and the quality of mission capability throughout the fleet. At the good old bottom line, what these systems do is straightforward: they enable training and planning to be done at Strike and in the fleet, in minutes or a few hours, that would take days or even weeks if done manually, if the effort could even be attempted.

TAMPS console in terrain mode. Operator is Capt. John Blum, USMC.

Birds of Prey

"The men could never describe, even to one another, the feeling that flying gave them: a sense of perfection that only God—or maybe just bad luck—could take away."

—Jake Grafton, A-6 pilot, fictional character from *Flight of the Intruder,* by Stephen Coonts

Carrier air wings coming to Fallon seem alike on the surface, with fighters and attack aircraft, fixed-wing and helicopter support birds. The sights and sounds have a familiarity—the squadron markings differ, but the jet and turbo-prop engines are the same, the paint schemes for most of the aircraft are all variations in a theme of shadow blue-grey, and the flight suits and safety gear are strictly issue. Beneath this surface similarity, however, there is a world of difference.

Each air wing in the United States Navy is different—in numbers and in composition, in squadron home location and deployment, in history and temperament. East Coast air wings know different waters and weather from the wings of the West Coast. Each has its own favorite liberty locations—many squadrons have their "own" selected hangouts in ports within their cruise perspective. At Fallon, they face the identical training challenges, plotted by the Strike staff.

East Coast air wings sail the Atlantic, all the way from the Arctic Circle to South America, and cruise the "Med" routinely. They fly from their own familiar carriers, nuclear and conven-

tionally powered—*America* and *Kennedy, Eisenhower* and *Roosevelt, Saratoga* and *Lexington, Forrestal* and *Coral Sea* among them, sailing from home ports such as Norfolk, Virginia, or Jacksonville, Florida.

East Coast–based carrier battle groups can be found spending in-port periods during cruises at locations such as Naples in Italy, Palma de Mallorca, Malaga on Spain's south coast, the Israeli port of Haifa, Egypt's historic Alexandria—and even on an occasional visit to a Communist country such as Yugoslavia.

On the West Coast the arena is the vast Pacific, site of many epic WWII sea battles, from the Aleutians to the Antipodes, west into the Indian Ocean and Arabian Gulf. San Diego- or Alameda-based carriers include *Enterprise* and *Kitty Hawk, Ranger* and *Constellation, Carl Vinson* and *Nimitz.* West Coast wings, drawing squadrons from Whidbey to North Island, Lemoore to Miramar, spend time in Pearl Harbor, Hawaii; Perth, down under in Australia; and Hong Kong, Japan, Singapore, or the Philippines during WesPac cruises. It's a vast ocean.

Despite their many differences and similarities, every modern air wing rings variations on a theme of raw power carved from aluminum and titanium, tail hooks and squadron insignia, instruments and control systems, carbon-fiber and fiberglass composites, electronics and jet engines, bombs and missiles . . . and the hearts

Previous pages: And you thought the Alpha Strike was a thing of the past! Visiting air wing flexes fighter and attack muscle for the camera.

and minds, souls and motivation of the men and women who fly and maintain the wing's aircraft, no matter where they come from, regardless of where they call home. Women Navy pilots are not yet flying in the air wings but fly Aggressor and COD (carrier onboard delivery) aircraft. One Strike officer, recently retired, commented: "If women flew in the air wing today, I'd probably reenlist." Everyone is highly complimentary about the skill and motivation of the Navy's women pilots.

Strike will see all sixteen wings (fourteen ac-tive, two reserve) over an eighteen-month period. The task of Strike and its staff is to probe the strengths and weaknesses of each wing in power projection, bring them to cruise readiness, enable them to fight and win battles in the air. Unlike Top Gun, which caters to small and selected groups of Navy and Marine fighter pilots and is focused on ACM, every wing area of activity at every level of experience is tested in the Strike crucible.

The airplanes are the focal point: attack aircraft to deliver the heavy weapons, inflict pain on

ORGANIZATIONAL CHART

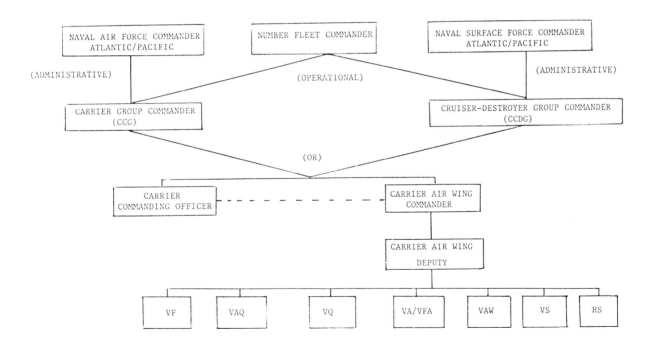

targets, and deliver antiradiation missiles to help the SEAD (suppression of enemy air defenses) effort; fighters to protect the bombers and interdict enemy thrusts at the fleet; and AEW, EW, ASW, SAR (search-and-rescue), and COD aircraft for vital support functions, without which neither the fighters nor the bombers could succeed.

ATTACK BIRDS

Attack planes used to lack the fighters' primal, predatory power—lumpish, not embodying the swagger, dash, innate killer instinct bred into the fighters, exemplified by the men who fly them. Fighters have been glorified by the media, the pilots made larger than life. Don't believe their PR? Ask them, and they will tell you. But even they realize that the wing's attack aircraft are no less vital, are the very reason for the carrier battle group's existence—to project Navy power, inflict damage on land or at sea. The birds are the F/A-18, A-6, and A-7.

—F/A-18 HORNET
When the F/A-18 Hornet came aboard, all the jibes about attack aircraft went out the scuttles. The Hornet is beautiful, but it can sting with devastating power—as both attack airplane and fighter.

Like the F-4 that came before it, the Hornet is multimission. The F-4 was a Navy aircraft

Strike instructors head Downtown carrying Mark 82s, Zunis, and several thousand rounds of twenty-mike-mike.

from McDonnell, developed from the initial interceptor role carrying AIM-7 Sparrows and AIM-9 Sidewinders by adding air-to-air gun and air-to-ground bombing attack capabilities. The F/A-18 was designed and produced from the start for dual roles.

The Hornet began life as Northrop's YF-17 lightweight fighter prototype, competing with the then-YF-16 as next-generation interceptor replacement for the F-4. When the F-16 won the DoD's "lightweight fighter" competition for Air Force use, the YF-17 became the Navy's

Lt. Comdr. Bill "Dawg" Shepherd, Strike's foremost Hornet expert, poses handsomely in school F/A-18.

choice—as the F/A-18. It is characterized by a HUD (head-up display)/HOTAS (hands-on throttle and stick)/all-electronic "glass" cockpit, two GE F404 afterburning engines, and the ability to sustain 9G as long as its pilot can.

How good is it? In development, the Hornet prototype was flown at Edwards in ACM by then-

Maj. (now Col.) Jim (''Black'') Lucas, Marine aviator extraordinaire, against the Tomcat. How did he do? Did he like it? How big a grin did he have to show you? ''I was used to having F-14s beat up on me [in the A-4 and F-4], especially in the corners and in the vertical. The Hornet can really make your eyes water with its performance—it has terrific corner velocity and can take a Turkey in ACM and then turn round and deliver ordnance as well or better than an A-6 [the Marine heavy attack bird]. A double punch.''

It can only get better. P^{3}I (preplanned product improvement) programs under consideration by the Navy for the Hornet, but not confirmed as of early 1988, should add color cockpit displays and potentially 3,500 pounds more fuel to what is now the shortest-legged and most fuel-critical aircraft on the boat. New engine mods planned for the twin GE F404 afterburning jet engines

Camera pod view of F/A-18 Hornet.

(see also A-6F comments below) will give it even more power. And the continually evolving weaponry of the attack business will toughen up its already shattering punch.

The Hornet is an amazing sight on the cat or ashore just before launch, as the pilot stirs the stick for a final control check. Instead of just a pair of surfaces moving—say, opposing ailerons or stabilators—the whole damn lot changes position under the control of the digital flight-control system (FCS). It looks like a hummingbird with St. Vitus' dance: ailerons, flaps, slats, stabilators, and rudders flapping in the breeze. The FCS has yielded a danger that (among other mishaps) killed the skipper of VX-4, landing in rain and a considerable crosswind at Miramar. When he applied rudder to maintain runway centerline alignment, aileron displacement flipped his Hornet. Nevertheless, the F/A-18 is a fleet favorite among its growing roster of pilots.

—A-6 INTRUDER

The air wings' heavy attack workhorse? Grumman's A-6, an all-weather, two-seat (pilot, B/N) attack aircraft with an illustrious twenty-year record of escalating capability in -A, -B, -C, -D, and -E models, based on its ability to haul nine tons of weapons to targets over 1,000 miles away. "K" models pass gas for all the wing's aircraft, equipped with fuel tanks mounted on weapons stations to augment internal capacity.

The heart of the A-6 is its advanced weapons

Two-ship of A-6E Intruders awaiting their turn over Dixie Valley targets.

computer, vital to inflicting precise punishment on the enemy, to be upgraded in the A-6F with a larger and more powerful system. That new system will drive a ''glass'' cockpit very much like the Hornet's. New radar will be part of the ''F'' package, and there will be two more weapons stations on the wings.

To match increased gross weight, GE F404 engines will replace the PW J52 turbojets used in earlier A-6s and EA-6s. In the interim, Pratt & Whitney has devised an upgrade for the J52 that would increase its thrust from 11,200 to

EA-6B Prowler lifts easily out of Fallon slinging two radar jammers, two fuel tanks, and a TACTS data pod.

12,000 pounds, a worthwhile improvement that will be accompanied by 20 percent faster spool-up. One of the few external differences with the ''F'' is its slightly enlarged engine air intakes just aft of the cockpit. Common engines with the Hornet will simplify carrier maintenance and logistics, always a concern on cruise despite the

COD for emergency bits and pieces. The extra weapons racks on the A-6F will enable the Intruder to defend itself with Sidewinders and the AMRAAM (Advanced Medium Range Air-to-Air Missile).

At press time, under debate was purchase of 150 A-6Fs, the prototypes of which have already flown, versus purchase of the ATA (advanced tactical aircraft), not due in the fleet until century's end at the earliest. In fact, the ''F'' seemed likely to fall to cost cutters' knives as the politicians attempted to balance the budget. The ''E'' remains deadly, especially low-level and at night, which are its specialties.

Want more? Read *Flight of the Intruder,* Stephen Coonts' great book about the A-6 in 'Nam. But realize as you read it that Coonts, on a Fallon DET, once landed his A-6 at the Fallon *municipal* airport, a few miles north of NAS Fallon. It took a heart-stopping launch for the squadron skipper to get the bird home from the short (4,000-foot) runway, with minimum fuel.

—A-7 CORSAIR

Still in service after two decades, flown by the Navy, Air Force Reserve, and Air National Guard in six models through the latest A-7E, Vought's A-7 is the quintessential light attack aircraft, able to carry 15,000 pounds of pain-inflicting weapons that include Sidewinders and a Vulcan cannon. The A-7 was a workhorse of the Vietnam period and acquitted itself admirably with very low loss rates.

A-7 unloads 1,000 pounds worth of high explosive over target complex.

Two-seat TA-7 flies dash-two with single-seater under wintry Nevada sky.

''Maverick'' bends his Tomcat around Fairview Peak during the filming of *Top Gun*. Low-level scenes were all shot at Fallon.

Although the Hornet is slowly replacing it throughout the wings, the appearance of the SLUF (Short Little Ugly Fucker) goes against it. Yet the high-wing and low-nose jet intake owe much of their aerodynamics to the great ''tits machine'' of post-WWII naval aviation from the same factory, the Chance-Vought F-8U. The SLUF will hardly win any beauty contests but is nevertheless appreciated by pilots for its ruggedness and its new weapons-delivery avionics and computer, and its color map display—a first with the fleet—of where you are

''Maverick'' bends his Tomcat around Fairview Peak during the filming of *Top Gun*. Low-level scenes were all shot at Fallon.

and where you are headed. And the A-7 avoids a couple of amusing characteristics of its F-8U predecessors—the Crusader's engine thrust line tended to push it *lower* on the glide slope when power was applied, say, on final for the boat(!), and the combination of low departure angle and minimal deck clearance of the F-8U made it attitude sensitive on recovery. The F-8U's characteristic 7-degree variable-incidence wing is also not retained in the A-7.

Corsairs deliver the goods: the latest avionics derivations permit precise dive, loft or toss bomb delivery. The fuel-thrifty TF41 turbofan engines, although not the world's most powerful or reliable power plants, give the A-7 speed up to Mach .92 and excellent attack range. ''K'' models pass gas for the wing, from fuel tanks carried on pylons under each wing, on weapons stations, as with the KA-6 bird.

FIGHTING BIRDS

The air wings that come to Strike at Fallon bring their fighters with them. Fighters these days are the F-14 Tomcat or the F/A-18 Hornet flown as a fighter.

F/A-18 and F-14 line up on waist catapults of USS *Ranger*. Note stabilator deflection of Hornet for cat takeoff.

—F-14 TOMCAT

Grumman's Mach 2+ Turkey does it all as a fighter—CAP; interceptions with its four Sparrows, four Sidewinders, and 20-mm Vulcan cannon; and the "one-versus-many" ACM that only its six Phoenix air-to-air missiles can tackle. The F-14 is the only U.S. fighter to carry the Phoenix. And for photoreconnaissance, a TARPS pod makes it a potent aerial spy. With its two-man crew, it is a deadly combination of speed, power, and weaponry, currently in the process of being upgraded in the "D" model with bigger engines for which it was originally designed and new cockpit avionics matching the Hornet's. With the new GE engines, the Tomcat will be able to go off the cat at max gross without burner, adding a useful increment of endurance to match the improved acceleration and resistance to compressor stall (no matter how impatient the pilot is with the throttle!).

Probably the only two things an F-14 driver dislikes about his work are single engine failures on the cat and flap slat lockout. ("I don't care much for flat spins," adds an F-14 driver, and what he does not add to his comment is that after three turns, as the NATOPS [Naval Air Training and Operations program] manual explains in attention-getting detail, the canopy may not detach and may inhibit egress.) Engine failures can ruin your day, and the Tomcat sports nine feet between thrust lines. On burner (with the old engines, before the "D" reaches the fleet), off the cat at max gross, it takes instant reflexes to unload and recover on one engine. (Yes, it has been done, but a lot of "pull"—gotta stay away from the water, right?—maybe the last thing the pilot does before taking the emergency egress. If he has time.)

Comdr. John Ed Kerr, recently skipper of VF-302, the F-14 reserve squadron at Miramar, suffered the indignity of losing an engine on the cat. Fortunately he was at carqual (carrier qualification) fuel state (about 8,000 pounds). "I'd glommed some of the videos showing loss of an engine on the cat. Pilots who were 'pulling' to get away from the water usually took a swim. The ones who unloaded the bird, cleaned it up, and flew away in 'ground' [water] effect, seemed to keep it together . . . that looked like the way to go." He came back to talk about it.

Flap-slat lockout occurs when wingtip and root sensors detect a more than 3-degree difference between flap-slat torque drive angle (translation: the chance of torque-shaft damage). When this happens, the flap-slat actuation system freezes and can be reenabled only by pulling a few fuses and retrimming manually (say, for recovery!). Tedious.

Flap-slat lockout? Yes. When the F-14 was originally designed, it not only had the high-speed advantage of swept wings but coupled leading-edge slats and trailing-edge flaps on the wing that enable it to fly slowly for recovery. Wing sweep and flap-slat actuation are slaved automatically to angle of attack. Almost the first day the Turkey zipped its way into an ACM encounter, the driver realized that the increased lift of the "curled" wing made the F-14 a better fighter. Pull, and they curled; push, to "extend," and they unloaded nicely and let the bird accelerate.

Aggressor A-4 lineup at Fallon. Paint schemes represent a spectrum of potential Commie and Third World bad guys.

But ACM is invariably a split-second pull-push-pull proposition, and the system can occasionally get wound around its own axle (or torque drive-shaft).

AGGRESSOR BIRDS

Aggressor aircraft have been used since before the inception of Top Gun during the 1969–72 reprieve from the North Vietnam air war. Originally a grab-ass business that came logically from the eagerness of fighter jocks to hassle, Aggressors now formally simulate "enemy" aircraft with their own specialized aircraft, squadrons, and training. They expose fighter pilots—and now all air wing pilots at Strike—to the appearance and behavior of the kinds of adversaries they could expect to confront in the event of hostilities. The same concept has been used for years at Red Flag.

But technology on the other side of the Iron Curtain has not stayed in place. New and advanced fighters (and bombers) are being churned out in volume. As the 1990s loom, new Aggressor aircraft with capabilities matching those of the latest and most capable Warsaw Pact aircraft are joining ACM furballs and knife fights throughout the United States and at allied venues in Europe and the Far East.

As recently as the mid-1970s, the Soviets hardly trained their fighter pilots for ACM. Soviet

Aggressor pilot Lt. Comdr. Roger "Muff" Dadiamoff—an honest-to-God Russian—poses with his A-4E.

pilot Viktor Belenko, well known to many Strike staff and wing aviators, flew his MiG-25 from the Soviet Union to the civilian air base at Hakodate, on the northern Japanese island of Hokkaido, in 1976 and has become a valued consultant to the Navy.

He tells the inside story: "Soviet doctrinal response to a power projection was simple: recall all your fighters (the specific radio command was the single word 'CARPET'), then detonate a nuclear device or devices at 50,000 feet to neutralize the entire incoming force." He shrugs and smiles: "Yes. It would almost certainly mean taking out quite a few of your own aircraft, who would not have completed their recoveries, but that is not a Soviet concern."

Today, in an uneasy world, Warsaw Pact and Third World countries flying Soviet-made aircraft may have to fight conventionally, including classic ACM. The latest Soviet fighters have the capability. These are the adversaries that the United States and its allies could face in many places around the world.

Aggressor aircraft usually outperform conventional fleet equivalents, because except for the TACTS wiring they are stripped of weapons and are often (e.g., in the renowned A-4 "Mongoose") reengined for extra go. Hot rods, no less.

Today there are even Reserve Aggressor squadrons, matching the successful efforts of then-SecNav John Lehman to establish Reserve air wings (one on each coast) with capabilities close in almost all respects (or so say the Reserves) to the regular wings.

—F-16N

Newest, baddest Navy Aggressor is the F-16N,

based on the General Dynamics F-16A/B/C/D, thousands of which are now in allied service throughout the world. The F-16N entered service as an Aggressor with Top Gun, at Miramar, in fall 1987. It duplicates closely the capabilities air wings can expect to see in the Fulcrum and Flanker fighters from the USSR and Warsaw Pact countries—high Mach, rapid acceleration, high sustained corner velocities, vaulting vertical authority, excellent maneuverability, ultramodern weapons systems . . . plus the ability to sustain

8–9G. It will replace not only the A-4s and F-5s that have been used as Aggressors, but the few Israeli Kfirs—a Mirage clone that was developed by the Israelis from purloined plans—that have found their way to Oceana's ACM school on loan from Israel.

Welcome to the nineties. GLOC (G-induced loss of consciousness) and hemorrhoids for the Aggressor pilots. And for fighter pilots in the wings. Same old story.

Aggressor pilots accustomed to the old F-5 and A-4 birds, with their limitations on power, speed, and the view outside, are raving about the F-16 and its incredible capabilities, including that huge, clear canopy without frame that provides a view as big as all outdoors. The side-stick controller takes little time to master and

Top Gun and Navy Aggressor F-16Ns at Miramar will sock it to the air wings as no F-5E could.

enjoy, even for pilots (they are in the majority) to whom a center stick has been the norm throughout their flying lives.

There's another neat trick buried inside the F-16N's computer: envelope variable in software. The digital flight-control system, or FCS, can be reprogrammed with less control authority, to reduce aircraft roll and pitch rate and other abilities, and thus simulate lesser adversaries.

—F-5E/F TIGER

Don't overlook the F-5, the tiny, agile, and deadly little fighter cooked up by Northrop lo these many years ago, flown by pilots of more than twenty nations around the world. Either in single-seat "E" or two-seat "F" versions, with leading-edge maneuvering slats to complement the trailing-edge wing flaps, the Tiger is a tiger—tough to see (especially against the ground), hard to turn against with its 7.4G limit (vs. the 6.5G limit of the F-14, a small but critical difference), lacking only brute power with its two small GE J86 turbojet engines. If you're up against a well-flown F-5, mister, you're in big trouble.

—A-4 SKYHAWK

You'll still find many single- and two-seat A-4 adversaries, wearing bizarre camouflage that blends them maddeningly with sky or ground, in regular and Reserve units at Fallon. All have been reengined and stripped to make them re-

markably capable in the vertical, even against much more powerful and modern adversaries. And they're agile as can be, considering their age. Or even not considering their age.

Properly flown—as it almost always is by eager Aggressor pilots—Heineman's Hotrod can make ACM life hell for a Tomcat or Hornet

Single- and two-seat A-4 Mongooses on Fallon flight line prior to Aggressor ACM hop.

95

driver, flying much newer technology, who is caught behind the power curve or asleep at the stick with his energy down. For an A-6 or A-7 attack pilot, escape is the only realistic solution. Haul ass—right now, or sooner. No excuses are necessary. The alternative: a kill.

Earlier emphasis on training with Aggressors for 1-v-1, 1-v-2, 2-v-2, and other limited ACM engagements is now giving way to concerns about multibogey (1-v-many or 1-v-unknown) scenarios, and with the latest missiles that have greatly expanded ''aspect,'' further emphasis is being given to head-on engagements—first shooter wins. As ''Wigs'' Ludwig, recent Top Gun skipper, puts it: ''You probably won't get a second shot.''

AEW, EW, AND ASW BIRDS

Advanced early warning, electronic warfare, and antisubmarine missions are vital to carrier battle group security and mission success. Air wings rely on them, and even the most chauvinistic fighter or attack pilot knows how much they really mean to mission success. How important is AEW? Many nations worldwide are getting into AEW, and the Brits wished they'd had it in the Falklands!

—E-2C HAWKEYE (AEW)
Continually upgraded over the years, the Grumman E-2C Hawkeye, or ''Hummer,'' is

E-2C Hawkeye provides airborne early warning and command/control for the carrier air wing.

97

the electronic eyes and ears of the carrier battle group. This ungainly looking but effective aircraft is able to roam hundreds of miles from the carrier, and with its electronics systems—distinctive radome with sensitive, 360-degree radar—it can find, identify, track, and analyze hundreds of potential threats at once, over land or water, in as much as three million cubic miles of airspace from the surface of the ocean to the edges of space. In a word: awesome.

Hummers also handle strike/interceptor control, surface surveillance or SAR coordination, and communications relay.

With its crew of two pilots up front and three electronics specialists (CICOs) in back, and twin fuel-efficient turboprop engines, the E-2C can work for hours on station—in high-threat situations, the wing will keep an E-2C aloft around the clock by rotating its aircraft.

Today, along with its sister C-2 COD aircraft from Grumman (passengers, freight, no radome), this is the only propeller-driven aircraft on the carrier, and pilots going off and on the boat are proud of their ability to handle the challenging, three-axis "P" effects absent in the "easy-to-fly" pure-jet aircraft. The flight line at Fallon always sees E-2s when wings are TAD, standing tall and sprouting their props and straight wings proudly.

—A-3/EA-3 (SPECIAL MISSIONS)

With more than thirty years' continuous service under its belt, and designed in the 1940s as the XA3D-1, Douglas Aircraft's twin-jet EA-3/A-3 Skywarrior, or "Whale" (forty tons at max gross!), is the wings' oldest surviving flying machine. And what an amazingly versatile beast it has turned out to be: starting as the Navy's

only carrier-based long-range bomber, it has been pressed into service as photorecon airplane, ESM/ECM platform, tanker, and trainer, and, in the seventies and eighties, a system for "special mission support" (don't you just love their euphemisms!).

The favorite bumper sticker of this group (what else?): "Save the Whales." It may not be possible. Most of the fleet birds still active have piled up much more than the expected airframe hours. Their patches are patched, and the way this ele-

gant antique creaks, groans, and bends *visibly,* exterior skin flexing and rippling during a cat stroke, makes strong men look away in dismay. It tends to break on recovery, too.

In late November 1987 the Navy decided that the Whale should no longer operate from the boat because of its advanced age and, in some cases, the inexperience of its pilots, which gave rise to safety concerns. Despite this decision, the birds will remain flyable and a select group of pilots carqualed in case of need.

—S-3 (ASW)

Lockheed's twin-turbofan-powered S-3, with its crew of four (pilot, copilot, tactical coordinator, acoustic-sensor operator), is the fleet's premier long-range ASW bird. Properly the Viking, dubbed the Hoover (hear its twin turbofans and you understand the nickname instantly), the

Save the whales! Huge A-3 Skywarrior is still used for tanker and electronic intelligence missions.

99

S-3 is the on-board complement to the land-based P-3 Orion.

The Viking is not particularly fast (a mere 450 knots), but with its thrifty General Electric TF-34-GE-400 turbofans it can range up to 2,000 nautical miles and carry torpedoes, depth bombs, conventional bombs, the Harpoon missile, rockets, and mines. Its ASW sensor system and powerful on-board computing capabilities make it deadly to hostile subs, including conventional, high-speed, deep-diving, and quiet-running boats.

—EA-6B PROWLER (EW/ECM)

Grumman's massive Prowler—thirty tons on the catapult at maximum gross takeoff weight—was developed from the A-6 in the early 1970s. Its purpose: to practice the arcane art of EW (electronic warfare), to listen for and jam enemy radars and associated physical threats. The basic A-6 airframe was lengthened to accommodate two more crew—electronic countermeasures officers, or ECMOs. Its only flying shortcoming: a tendency to "bury" that long, heavy nose, calling for lots of care at low altitudes.

By 1988 the Prowler had gone through its fifth major upgrade, with no end in sight. Indeed, the aircraft has become the focus of wing tactics, as electrons have started to become almost as important as bombs and bullets (see TEAMS system description in Chapter Four). A Prowler can blast electronic holes in the most menacing IADS, which will let lots of ordnance-bearing

EA-6B Prowler is slated to carry Harpoon antiship missiles. One is shown here on outboard station.

SH-3 Sea Knight helo provides close-in ASW coverage as well as search-and-rescue for the carrier birds.

attack aircraft in for their deadly play. The aircraft has its counterparts in the EF-111 Raven (jamming only) and F-4G Wild Weasel birds (jamming and attack on radiating targets) flown by the Air Force.

The primary Prowler weapon is the ALQ-99 ESM/ECM system, carried in up to five wing pods (pods are selected and varied based on the air-defense threat against which the specific mission is directed). The three ECMOs (the right front and the two rear closets) work their magic through a set of computers and display screens that look a little like the CRTs of your home computer but take years of training to master effectively.

The next Prowler? Probably a multiseat version of the ATA, when the advanced tactical aircraft eventually reaches the fleet.

—SH-3 (ASW)

Fixed-wing pilots—heavily in the majority aboard the boat and ashore—like to poke good-natured fun at the helo drivers ("if God had intended man to fly like that, She would have made birds with wings rotating on top of their heads," etc.). Behind the whimsy, the fact is that many of the former owe their lives to the latter when working in SAR mode, and both groups are well aware of the fact.

The SH-3 Sea King (no affectionate nickname) is basically a four-man ASW bird for close-in submarine detection in support of the carrier battle group, with its sonar, sonobuoys, and associated systems. But it can also carry thirty-one paratroopers in troop-lift role, fifteen stretchers and a medical attendant in medevac work, and up to twenty-five survivors in SAR activities. SH-3s shadow the boat during launch and recovery to pluck from the sea any unfortunate fixed-wing aviator who may have a problem off or on the boat. Ask the insufferable wise guys and they will finally admit to you how much the SH-3 is appreciated.

From all of these elements, air wings are forged. But then there are the hard weapons they carry, which form the real power in Navy power projection.

SUPPORTING CAST OF CHARACTERS

The boat, the birds, and the aircrew are front and center, the focus of the mind and eye. But none of them could function without the support from the specialists who serve them.

They number in the tens of thousands, those unsung heroes—from the flight-deck crew who risk their lives daily in one of the most physical activities on earth to the aerospace industry engineers and Navy test pilots who create and test the airframes, from the engine and electronics technicians who work untold hours to keep the aircraft up, to the black-shoe Navy that runs the carriers central to the Navy's worldwide power projection.

Nowhere is this more true than at Strike, a serious flying billet for most of the staff. The expanding Strike complement of A-6, A-7, TA-7, and F/A-18 birds relies for flight readiness on a dedicated team of a score or more maintenance specialists, supported where necessary by contract staffs working on site and by the manufacturers' representatives from airframe, engine, and avionics suppliers. The airplane drivers may be the "rock stars" of modern military aviation, but they couldn't fly without the ground team and they know it!

Warriors

"Only the spirit of attack, born in a brave heart, will bring success to any fighter aircraft, no matter how highly developed it may be."

—Adolf Galland, Luftwaffe ace, September 1939

Warriors! Make no mistake. Don't underestimate them. Never try to sell them short or misunderstand their intentions. They are warriors. By choice. By profession. By action. This is a special breed. To them the spirit of attack is as natural as breathing. Whatever their level, they are involved—aircrew or support personnel, technicians or officers, ashore or afloat, they are in it up to their eyebrows.

These men and women, in their khakis or flight suits or dress uniforms, wearing regulation shades and zipped lips, or standing at the O-Club or enlisted bar in their civvies, are warriors in a cold-war world that often heats to melting point. The tip of the spear.

The pilots represent an interesting challenge to the chain of command. Give them their heads, and they'll try to fly in the twilight zone; crush them, and the fire goes out. For the chain of command from training on, within the squadrons, on the boat or ashore, all the way to the CAG and his own set of constraints, it's a balancing act between the vital internal forces of courage and will and the inevitable external realities of restraint and maturity.

Try to civilize them if you can, tame them with diplomacy, statesmanship, treaties, peace pacts, or a war of words stretching around the globe, but beneath that veneer they are warriors. For them there is no alternative. That is what they are paid to be, that is what they have chosen to be, and that is what the Navy expects of them. At Fallon, at Strike, and in daily fleet operations at hot spots worldwide, the Navy demands nothing less. Often a lot more.

Vice Adm. James Stockdale—Gulf of Tonkin eyewitness, Vietnam POW for seven long years, Strike community leader, now Hoover Institution Fellow—said it well in his memorable 1965 comments as air wing commander en route to do battle in Vietnam. He said, in part:

Once you go "feet dry" over the beach, there can be nothing limited about your commitment. "Limited" war means to us that our target list has limits, our ordnance loadout has limits, our rules of engagement have limits, but that does not mean that there is anything "limited" about our personal obligations as fighting men to carry out assigned missions with all we've got.

So these men, and the women who work with them, as well as those who support them at home under the pressure of their own special and inescapable rigors, have no illusions about the name of the game, the nature of the business.

The nature of the over-all business is war, the task of the battle group in general and the air wing in particular is to project naval power, and the name of the individual game is commitment. Some have handed in their wings of gold when that personal commitment failed them. No

A-6E Intruder can carry up to nine tons of various ordnance, as much as the biggest strategic bombers of World War II.

one speaks of it, but each knows in his heart and mind that the warrior's test comes . . . daily. How does Strike fit into a naval aviator's life?

At Strike the task is to train air wings to succeed at the business of war. How do they do it? The program really goes back in time, to each individual air wing the day it is formed. The Strike DET has become vital, absolutely integral to the training cycle and to the cruise.

THE TRAINING CYCLE

An air wing recycles itself under the leadership of a new CAG each eighteen months, typically, the last six months of which are spent on cruise. The last major precruise evolution is the Strike

Flight surgeon/RIO Connie ''Doc'' Ward in the back-seat of a VF-302 Tomcat.

DET. Sometimes that year of preparation for the cruise may be compressed into as short as five to six months, in time of emergency, especially if the wing comprises experienced squadrons manned by a high proportion (60 percent or more) of old hands who have worked and flown together and a limited proportion of "nuggets," or inexperienced junior officers who are not fully up to speed in carrier ops. There are times when the cruise starts suddenly and lasts indefinitely.

One Strike staff officer tells of being called during a Mediterranean crisis and told he'd be gone "for a couple of weeks at most." He recalls: "It was New Year's Day. I had the worst hangover of my life. My wife was pregnant, due in a week, and she drove me to where the MAC [Military Airlift Command] C-141 was leaving. I couldn't tell her where we were going. We were Whidbey's best-prepared Prowler squadron, just finished with CARQUALs.

"They flew us initially to Spain. We were gone seven months on that 'couple of weeks' DET. It cost a lot of marriages."

By the time recycle training is over, the wing should be ready to go to war. Work starts at

A-6 drops Mark 82 "Snakeyes" over Dixie Valley. Note retarder vanes deploying on first bomb.

the grass roots, building competence and confidence—senior pilots take nuggets and watch them "at work," evaluate their skills, assess their strengths and weaknesses—in effect, become their mentors, to pass on the accumulated wisdom of the years. The bottom line: the mission.

MISSION PLANNING

Every day, strike leaders and planners—fleetwide, as well as at Strike—must put it all together and create an effective mission plan. The task is multidimensional, whether a small contingency task or a major evolution involving many aircraft.

The diverse elements of a well-planned "strike package" include the following (and you thought that Top Gun was all there was—go on, admit it!). This is the aviator's time to think, and think hard, so that as much as possible is known—eventualities have been anticipated, unknowns minimized. Note: everything affects everything.

The bullshit stops here. Most of air wing attends post-hop TACTS debrief of strike mission.

—OVERALL STRIKE OBJECTIVE

The Strike leader and attack-element group must know the primary and secondary targets and define the TOT (time over target). The military objective must be clearly specified—is this a punitive or retaliatory strike, and what is the PK (probability of kill) demanded of the strike group?

Target study is exacting. The strike group must have the description, type of construction, location and elevation, and local topography and terrain features. Can the target be seen visually, on FLIR (forward-looking infrared), on radar? Weather counts, so forecasts must be available, in enough detail (as specific WX [weather report] elements) to note conditions at launch—over the target and on recovery, contrail levels, even target density altitude—that will affect strike aircraft ordnance-carrying and maneuvering capability, and the ability of that ordnance (e.g., glide weapons, such as LGBs [laser-guided bombs] and Walleyes) to fly. TOT affects ambient light levels, sun angle, terrain and target shadows, cockpit reflections and distortion, which will also determine the best run-in direction with respect to terrain.

—INTEL SOURCES AND REQUESTS

Beyond target data (see above), intel can make huge differences between success and failure. Within the battle group itself, intel will come from TARPS, EA-3, EA-6B, and other wing aircraft, including S-3/SH-3 data on enemy submarines affecting the battle group's course/position, shipboard RDF (radio direction finding) giving vital data on enemy radiating/communicating sources, and satellite information.

Intel from outside the battle group can be vital

S-3A Viking coming aboard carrier.

(better initiate requests ASAP!), depending on target(s). All this intel must be accumulated, measured, prioritized. Everything really affects everything, in a matrix of data and decisions that has hundreds, or more likely thousands, of nodes and as many interpretations.

—FRIENDLY ORDER OF BATTLE

Battle group disposition is important. Among the considerations: What are the fleet air-defense posture and the antiair, surface, and subsurface ROE status? Are CV air operations in cyclic or flex-deck mode? As the Strike *Planner's Guide* puts it: "Who is out there on our side? How do we keep from getting shot down by our own people?"

Rules of engagement—ROE. Ah, yes. Key to mission procedure. Again, from the trusty *Guide:* "How can we engage the enemy? Air to air, air to mud (and not forgetting EW ROE)? Are there any ROE limitations on what weapons we can use? Are there things near the target we can't bomb? Can civilian or third-party casualties be accepted?" Harsh realities? Yes. War is hell.

—ENEMY ORDER OF BATTLE

Strike calls enemy threats to the strike group the main factor in creating mission plans. How well a planner figures out with what the enemy is going to shoot, from where it will come, and

Tomcat and Marine Corps F/A-18 are joined by Aggressor A-4E after a bit of friendly jousting over Dixie Valley.

how to defeat it will determine, to a great extent, strike success. Is it an integrated threat or fighters under group-controlled intercept with autonomous SAM and AAA threats?

What sort of enemy ocean surveillance exists? How effective are his air-defense system, his EW activity, his ESM and ECM? Where will his fighters come from? How many, and what type/performance/ordnance can be expected? SAM, AAA, and small arms? What about the psychological and sociological factors—political and military stability and leadership, relations with neighboring countries? Will nonlocal troops be involved (Cubans, Eastern European Communists, etc.), with their own way of fighting? How can we beat the threats?

—WEAPONEERING

A useful coined word, weaponeering. It means everything that the ordnance must do to meet mission objectives: desired PK (probability of kill), type, number and delivery for maximum effectiveness, range versus payload on the particular aircraft, fin/fuse configurations, arming and delay times.

The boat is a factor. What ordnance is available? And what does it take to break out, build up, and load on the strike aircraft (remember the 1983 Lebanon strike with aircraft ordnance loadout versus time over target?)? It has become a major issue, with ancillary but essential matters such as drop-tank use, FLIR, TARPS, or Walleye control pods, MER/TER (multiple-ejection-rack/ triple-ejection-rack) space or potential aircraft reconfiguration.

Every mission is different, everything interconnected. Skill, experience, and leadership are the issues. Decide, now!

—THREAT SUPPRESSION AND NEUTRALIZATION

Avoid threats if possible; bust them in the mouth if necessary. That's how to get ordnance on the real target. A strike pilot will fly over, under, or around threats, sometimes sacrificing a maximum bomb load to get an extra, lifesaving 50 knots versus known threats. Wingies are sometimes the most reliable RHAW (radar homing and warning system).

—STRIKE PACKAGE

The complete assembly of assets ends up as a strike package, the planner's best work on how to achieve his mission objective. These days, with Strike at work and training the wings, putting the package together is seen as a core skill, and an individual officer's ability to wrap his mind around the task is measured critically. He gets to demonstrate that skill at Strike and on the cruise.

Convincing fake: fiberglass target simulates Soviet ground-to-air missile system. Ranges are studded with such artful counterfeits.

Wave-off at night aboard USS *Ranger*. Note last-second corrections in flight path. The pucker factor is never higher for Navy pilots (long exposure exaggerates light level).

—TO THE TARGET AND BACK

Final and critically important mission details must now be planned and timed with precision measured in seconds—launch, comm, rendezvous/tanking, formations, ingress, pop/roll-in/aimpoints, and ordnance delivery on the target at the correct TOT, without being fragged, egress and return, then that adrenalin-producing recovery on the boat.

SAR/RESCAP considerations come into play now: What are the battle group's SAR assets (SEALs; submarines; any local Army, Air Force, or Marine units; allied or other friendly ground forces)?

Escape and evasion must be covered: Are there known safe areas, and what heading would be taken from the target by a damaged aircraft unable to return to the boat? Where are friendlies or partisans, and possible rendezvous or pickup points? What about contact or broadcast times and primary/secondary radio frequencies? It's all related to over-all mission success.

—NOW: BRIEF IT!

With all these activities considered, documented, revised, and evaluated—to a typically compressed time schedule and endless fill-in-the-blanks uncertainties—these are the data that must be communicated up the chain of command for review, discussion, and (dis)approval, then to all strike-group elements via detailed briefing. At any level, from junior officer to squadron skipper, it's a challenge! Personal communications skills count.

That's what Strike is all about. For the warrior, it's a lifetime of work and commitment, compressed into the three-week Strike DET. It's a set of considerations to fight by, to win by . . . to live or die by.

THE CRUISE

After Strike, on the cruise, these are the naval aviator's daily chores—the planning and execution of effective mission briefs. But then, after all the paperwork has been done and the strike flown in theory, it must be executed in practice.

For the modern warrior in the fleet, the flying is at the bottom and on top of it all—the basic urge to excel at the raw art of carrier aviation, the single most challenging set of flying skills in the world. Yet the flying must be autonomic, so that flying right is as natural as breathing. The complicated technological assemblage, in which a minor problem can escalate into sudden death, must become transparent to the pilot.

Sudden death. We don't talk about that sort of thing, right? Right! But at its root that's what carrier flying is all about—transcendence and visceral reward, or potential nothingness. Strike trains at Fallon, but life is on the boat.

Rules to live by (courtesy Strike, and often written in the blood of fallen comrades, as Strike's staff reminds the reader):

- Speed is life—more is better.
- Be unpredictable—vary tactics, profiles, altitudes, routes/times, and don't fly roads, rivers, railroads.
- Never fly at lead's six o'clock, but maintain mutual support.
- Be inconsistent on pop/roll-in/pull-off (no repeat runs: one pass and haul ass).
- Don't radiate prematurely.
- Triple-check combat checklists.

- Don't duel with SAM/AAA sites!
- Keep your head on a swivel—the SAM/MiG you don't see gets you.
- Be aware of/avoid frag patterns.
- Use surprise and deception and FIGHT DIRTY!!!
- Know terrain elevation—the ground has a PK of 1.0, but SAMs, AAA, and fighters are less.
- In final run, you're on government time.
- KISS!

NIGHT TRAPS

Provided nothing serious breaks, the warrior at the controls of his aircraft, and those accompanying him in the other seat or seats, must be having the best time one can have in public, fully dressed, without being arrested. True!

Except for night traps. Night traps never become easy or comfortable or mere technique and achievement. In good weather, with moderate seas, perhaps a moon offering a horizon, it's like the heart rate—under control (just), the test of righteous manhood.

Stick and throttle in hand, all gauges check OK. There's the LSO (landing-signal officer) on the horn, not saying much. There's the good old meatball (''Centered''). Check deck alignment (''Great. On centerline, and the burble in the lee of the island isn't a factor''), airspeed nailed, based on fuel state (''Hey, 4,000 pounds, we're fat'') and the angle-of-attack indexer (''No sweat. On speed, plus or minus a couple of knots''), and the instant-by-instant visual/visceral check of man and machine comes out positive. It's a piece of cake. Well . . . relatively.

But when the weather is bad, overcast, moonless, with deck motion sufficiently severe that they have to rig the MOVLAS (Manually Operable Visual Landing Aid System), and the warrior is running on close to empty, in mind and body, in nerve and in JP-5, wrung out by a brutal mission, it's different.

He's at the controls, pointing a ten-, fifteen-, or twenty-ton device moving at over 200 feet per second at a seething array of lights that move on three axes. He has been tested to his limit by the mission just flown, fuel state is nibbling at nothing, and a bolter or wave-off is exactly what he doesn't need—translation: hell on earth.

These are discoveries lying in wait for the Soviets, known to be establishing their own carrier operations and also known to have suffered tragic accidents and losses of men and aircraft in the process, still in its infancy compared with the Americans, the British, the French. ''Good luck to them.'' That's what former Navy Secretary John Lehman has said. ''It has taken us more than seventy years to get it right.''

For the staff at Strike, and for every aviator in the visiting air wings, the struggle to maintain top professional performance is an endless one.

So. Get the flying down to the point where it's a challenge that's under control—most of the time. Hit the books, hard, but don't neglect those social obligations. Get the mission work nailed, after months of impossibly long days and nights, to the degree that things come together in a way others can comprehend and are willing to follow. Succeed at Strike, above all.

There's more. Be endlessly energetic, just tough enough. Be a loyal follower with that right-on touch of skepticism and intelligent contribution. Be a decisive leader—iron fist in velvet glove—willing to make decisions and live with them but not above accepting suggestions from others. Always remain concerned for the well-being and morale of the lowliest among the support troops, who can help make—or break—the highest and mightiest. Make sure that luck is good, that the numbers roll right. Avoid incompetent leaders in the wrong place at the wrong time.

At stake for the today's warrior in the Strike community: his career.

No, his life.

"The U.S. Navy has [developed] its own naval aviation . . . with amazing skill and enterprise and on a gigantic scale."

—Britain's Admiral of the Fleet Lord Keyes, 1944

Fallon's flight line is much like a typical fleet flight deck—a maelstrom of controlled activity. From dawn to dusk, and increasingly through the night as Strike's overall system capabilities improve, the pattern resounds with the familiar shriek of jet engines wound tight, the whump-whump of afterburners lighting for a launch. The jet-engine howls are interspersed with the occasional whine of a turboprop or even the drone of piston engines (there are 0-2 FAC birds on site for various local purposes), the whoppa-whoppa-whoppa of helicopters.

Sights match sounds. The visiting pilot can be found in typical aviator pose, head back, hand shielding the sun, eyes to the sky, watching the fighters and attack aircraft in the 4G break as they arrive singly or in groups. On final, it is the traditional Navy/Marine approach—3 degrees to impact—in approved carrier style.

TIME TO FLY

Now it is time to go fly and fight, see close up, in person, front and center, what your average fleet attack and fighter pilot does for a living at Strike, how he does it, how it can be perceived

by the eyes, appreciated fully by the intellect, and—most of all—how it feels in the gut. Let it not be doubted for an instant that the modern attack and fighter aircraft is an intensely physical device.

The real mainstream flying action at Strike comes in two predominant forms: interdiction and attack on a target, and ACM as part of a combat air patrol. For interdiction and attack, the basic tools are attack airplanes, the A-6 (heavy) and A-7 (light) (see Chapter Five). In working up the book, a Vought A-7 Corsair II was used for the attack demos; for ACM, work was done in the most up-to-date fighting machine the Navy and Marines are flying these days, the McDonnell Douglas/Northrop F/A-18 Hornet. Both these aircraft, and other Strike machines, were used as photo platforms.

Associated activities—the F-14s for all their diverse roles, the E-2C Hawkeye for AEW work, electronic warfare in the EA-6B, ASW in the S-3, even the helicopters—all become part of the integrated strike solution. "An attack or fighter pilot ain't gonna get there alone, pal," explains "Steely" Dan Dealey emphatically.

Strike's own aircraft are used for tactics development, weapons assessment, and staff aircrew proficiency. Unlike Top Gun, Strike does not use its aircraft and staff as "professional bogeys." Since Strike teaches fleet tactics, these are the techniques that must be flown, rather than the threat role.

But to begin at the beginning . . .

Previous pages: A-7 SLUF unloads 5-inch Zuni. Large rocket shares motor with Sidewinder air-to-air missile.

NAS LEMOORE, JULY 1987

Perspective: before you strap on a Navy airplane you must go through the ritual hazing pilots of every nationality face: the current flight physical to make sure that your noncurrent body is up to speed, and that you have current (or new) ejection-seat indoctrination that can save your life in an emergency. All the tickets must be properly punched, every *i* dotted, each *t* crossed, reams of paper completed and signed off. No one is exempt.

The procedure is strictly codified, though, and the same set of paperwork, the identical prods of body, mind, and emotion, are conducted at every major NAS facility throughout the world. To an aviator, a doctor is as much a natural enemy as the enemy.

NAS Fallon has not yet installed its own flight physiology department or water/ejection-seat training facilities, so the nearest accessible activity must be used. In the case of the Northern California/Nevada area, this means Lemoore.

NAS Lemoore lies in the heart of the San Joaquin Valley, halfway between San Francisco and Los Angeles, equidistant from the Sierra Nevada to the east and the Pacific Ocean to the west. Aviators coming there for the first time are told that all four escape spots and liberty arenas are equally convenient, but what they really mean is that they are equally inconvenient— a four-hour drive. This is where the attack community came when NAS Moffett Field, in Silicon Valley, became too urbanized and citizen complaints of noise went off the Richter scale.

Here the cheerful team in flight physiology administers all the tests—sight, hearing, height and weight, cardiac function, and, in the final

Strike A-7 masks himself behind ridge line prior to pop-up.

session with the doctor, the good old finger wave. Verdict both for photographer and scribe: OK all round.

SAFETY

They claim that they want to keep you alive— that it's considered bad form by the Navy to waste taxpayers, even if they are only scribblers or photographers and thus basically expendable. So there are more tests and more training dedicated to survival.

They have you step into the pool off a high platform from which it hurts to look down, swim endlessly in full flight gear, crawl into your life raft, and disentangle yourself from the cunningly

Your intrepid scribe awaits engine start in backseat of F/A-18 at Fallon.

draped parachute that just "saved your life" after an ejection.

There's more: escape from two well-simulated drowning opportunities in the Dilbert Dunker, which is a close copy of a fixed-wing cockpit, upside-down and fifteen feet deep in the bottom of the pool, then four more from the equally well simulated helicopter passenger compartment that rolls upside-down in the pool the instant it hits the water, just like the real thing that has taken so many lives. The final two helo escapes are done blindfolded . . .

The ejection-seat shot (or shots) is/are benign by comparison, and you just know that the 3–4G you experience in the hydraulically powered trainer is nothing compared with what you'd get—15–20G for an instant from the real seat rocket—if you just had to step outside and really meant it. Ejection injuries are common.

In the case of the Hornet seat, the black-and-yellow face curtain handles atop the seat, and the side handles, both familiar to Martin-Baker seat users, have gone away. Ejection is by means of just the single crotch handle grasped firmly with both Nomex-gloved hands and pulled up decisively. In a high-G emergency situation, that crotch handle would be the easiest for the pilot to grab instantly (or sooner); indeed, there are many situations where reaching up to the face curtain would be virtually impossible because of high loads on the arms and body, despite the protection it affords the face and head in ejections at high Mach.

Two pins safetying the seat must be removed to energize the seat before launch and replaced after recovery to safety it. These are normally handled by the plane captain. For the crew, there is a lever, much like a sports-car parking brake for the right hand, activated just before the throttles are advanced for launch and deactivated after disengaging the hook (on the boat) or turning off the active runway (on land) after recovery.

Tickets punched, the visitors come to Strike and are scheduled into a full program for the various flight schedules. There are, Brodsky explains, to be several hops, only two of which are described here: one low-level training hop to show how interdiction and bomb delivery are done, and one ACM hop to see the Hornet and the ranges close up. All this flying has been incorporated into the normal training and proficiency schedule.

Lt. Comdr. Craig B. ("Slim") Henderson is a tall, thin young man with serious eyes and a measured way of speaking. Like the rest of the

Strike staff, he is glad that Strike is an operational flying job. It keeps him where an aviator belongs—in the cockpit, right hand on the stick, left hand on the throttle. His serious mien is a front: this is a man who derives great pleasure and satisfaction from his work as an attack pilot.

Strike's two TA-7Cs are part of an assemblage of nine aircraft that also include A-6Es, A-7Es, and F/A-18s (single seat). Having these aircraft at NSWC's disposal enables aircrew, all the way up to the skipper, to remain current. And the fact that they are flying almost daily is not lost on visiting wings, who tend to view with skepticism lectures from armchair warriors who might be long on theory and short on practice, or who only fly as bogeys. *En garde,* Top Gun. The Navy looks with envy at the Air Force Fighter Weapons School at Nellis, set up with an entire *wing* dedicated to Aggressor work!

Suiting up is the first order of priority, aided by one of the riggers who are on the contract maintenance team at Strike. Over the Nomex flight suit comes the G suit with air-hose connection dangling; the harness through which one is attached to the ejection seat; and the emergency-gear pack with radio, inedibles and water, smoke makers, mirror, and the remainder of the forty-pound yoke a modern military pilot carries to work. On the feet: steel-toed flight boots. For the head: the fiberglass-composite helmet with clear and smoked visors, plus oxygen mask.

We proceed from the rigging area carrying our helmets and check with the plane's crew chief at maintenance control. It's vital to survey the paper history of service for the particular bird we will be flying. It's ''up'' and ''up'' (airframe and avionics) with no serious gripes, but Slim notes the more-interesting past discrepancies and what was done about them. A couple or three queries, an equal number of straight answers, and he accepts the airplane.

''Walking down'' enables us to review the plan, based on our earlier brief. At the airplane, we poke, prod, and pry at all the obvious and some not-so-obvious places, checking a setting here, a switch there, a computer reading, the state of the tires, the absence of telltale red hydraulic fluid leaks from the vitals of the beast. Slim hangs with all his weight from both flaps but fails to dislodge them.

In the cockpit, we attach ourselves to the seat with the Koch fittings, cinch the straps tight, strap on the leg restraints that will pull our legs and feet tightly to the seat if we have to eject, plug in the O₂ and the air source for the G suit

Busy Fallon flight line with entire air wing in temporary residence.

125

on the console to the left and the microphone connection at the back of the neck that will link with external radio and the ICS (internal communications system) that lets us talk to each other.

Slim gets an engine start from the "huffer," or APU (auxiliary power unit), rolled up next to the bird, and the panel comes alive. Now we are committed, barring unforeseen problems. He waves the huffer away. Checklists, checklists—Slim calls down every item on the ICS to verify status, including essential backseat items, and calls the tower for a clearance. Our call sign: "Strike One."

At thousands of dollars per hour, every flight has a purpose. Our purpose today: VFR low-level nav and bombing, starting with a low-level penetration from the Pacific Ocean at Point Bravo all the way across Northern California into Western Nevada on low-level training route VR1250.

The VR1250 entry point shown on the sectional map is right on the ocean. The plan is to maintain max altitude of 200 feet AGL (above ground level) and an airspeed of 480 knots for about 200 miles, until VR1250 ends and spits us out at Pyramid Lake, just north of Reno, thirty miles northwest of Fallon.

Departure and cruise are routine, the clearances from Reno and Oakland ditto, relaxed as an airline flight but without the flight attendant to bring refreshments. As we climb, the heat of a low-level cockpit goes away and a comfortable coolness takes over. Military air-conditioning systems work well at altitude.

It is the calm before the storm. At 30,000 feet, we survey the forested hills and cultivated valleys below, knowing that in a few short minutes we will be down and dirty, in the weeds, simulating a penetration into an enemy target area.

Slim drops down below 18,000 feet and into uncontrolled airspace, advising ATC (air traffic control) of his intentions, until we cross the coast, roll inverted with throttle back, and descend to sea level in a smooth 3G split-S maneuver he times and executes flawlessly to bring us down to 200 feet above water level. His stick-and-rudder and throttle work are minimalist.

Advance the throttle, the airspeed indicator steadies at just under 500 knots; pick up the nose to 200 feet as we cross the coastline and go "feet dry" and then initiate the first of a series of maneuvers that will occupy our entire attention for thirty minutes—the low-level penetration.

The name of the game is terrain masking, using the mountains and valleys as hiding places into which line-of-sight radar cannot peer to illuminate us. Speed is life, and so is minimum altitude, and here Slim shows the form of a master. The HUD velocity vector shows us continually where the nose will go, cuing him to pull just enough to clear the next ridge line.

The ridges are aligned roughly north-south, but our route is east-west. So we must climb up and over, then burrow down into the weeds. Slim's technique, which he has prebriefed carefully and practiced for a thousand hours, is to pitch up slightly before the ridge, roll almost inverted a few hundred feet ahead of it, and then cross the ridge canopy to the trees or dirt at an angle, roll back wings level as we reach the valley floor, hugging the terrain closely, and then do it all over again. Our briefed 200-foot clearance is frequently less than fifty feet on ridge crests, guaranteed to minimize exposure to "enemy radar."

All this must be accomplished while maintaining a VFR course prescribed by the mission (in life, by the Federal Aviation Agency). Slim is helped in the A-7 by its map display, a system that incorporates a color map on 35-mm film that shows him where he is at all times, but he also navigates from a premarked sectional and his memory of the terrain.

The "pulls" are continual, endless, and violent—typically around 4–5G, but in some situations as much as 6.5–7G where we must descend into and pull up out of rugged ravines. Some of the time we are floating at close to zero G in our harnesses or pressed up against them, even feeling occasional helmet contact with the canopy in negative G. Cinch those straps tighter!

Five miles short of our exit point, without warning, it is suddenly too much for the backseater. The relentless pull-push-pull of a low-level penetration finally takes its toll. Even an empty stomach can scream for mercy. For the driver, it's less taxing because he knows what's coming second by second.

"Knock it off. Knock it off. Sorry, Slim. The mind is willing but the body is saying 'forget this shit.'" The ego is badly bruised, too, having to cry uncle—and so close to the end of the training mission.

"Roj." With a smooth, even 2G pull he vaults the A-7 over the last line of hills short of Pyramid Lake, and the backseater manages not to throw up into the oxygen mask. If this had been an actual penetration, the attack pilot would have flown so as to eliminate wing "flashes," much harder than our hop, and then he would have to find his target and hit it, despite fighters, AAA, SAMs, and other business-as-usual problems.

Two minutes later, after a brief interlude at a steady 1G and in the cool of a higher altitude, we are refreshed and recovered, ready to see how the A-7 delivers ordnance. "We flew 'clean,' without drag-producing ordnance under our wings," explains Slim. "Our fuel use has been moderate and gives us more time on the range. With a load of ordnance, we would have flown as much as forty knots slower and used 20 percent more gas." The A-7's turbofan, while lacking brute power, is thrifty enough to make the airplane an impressive long-range bomber.

Bombing, then. We slip past Fallon to the Gabbs MOA (military operating area), so that Slim can demonstrate the real work: shallow-angle delivery, followed by some vigorous escape maneuvers to "avoid AAA and SAMs," then steep delivery and "escape," pulling up to 7G in the corners, and the brutally physical side of attack work becomes abundantly clear. Gs need to be pulled daily to acquire a tolerance. Otherwise—hard work!

Then, to make it tougher, there is the pop up from low level, followed by a roll over to inverted while acquiring the target visually, roll back to wings level for delivery. Finally, over-the-shoulder delivery used with nukes: pull up hard from low level/high speed and toss from a carefully computed point in a steep climb. The escape: pull up some more, to the vertical, then all the way over the top, finally roll back wings level and accelerate down into the weeds at maximum speed. We have sampled the A-7 delivery repertoire.

The 4G break into the pattern is an anticlimax. Taxi, accept directions from the crew chief, park, chop the throttle. Silence. Disconnect O_2, G suit, and harness. Slim is already down beside the A-7 as the backseater climbs from the cockpit. Helmet off, he is smiling a tight smile.

"Nice hop."

"Roj that."

* * *

Two-seat TA-7 hunkers down amidst Sierra peaks for max stealth, lowest PK.

ACM in the Hornet. Any pilot with an interest in the Navy/Marine flying world knows about the Hornet and its awesome performance.

VFA-106 is a combined Marine/Navy FRS (fleet replacement squadron), still often called a RAG (replacement air group) by old-timers. The squadron is based at Cecil Field in Florida but keeps a permanent DET at NAS Fallon simply because it is a much better place to train pilots both in ACM and air-to-ground weapons delivery.

Maj. Vic ("Clam") Simpson, USMC, is XO, a compact man with round face and ready smile, black hair greying at the temples, a direct Marine Corps gaze into the soul of a mere civilian visitor. His flying career goes back fifteen plus years to the F-4 and A-4, well over 2,000 hours of fighter and attack work—close air support is a

128

Marine specialty. Marine aviators are multipurpose, like the Hornet itself: go off and on the boat or from land, fly fighter and attack missions, do whatever has to be done. Gary Larson's "Far Side" once portrayed an undersized dinosaur standing dejectedly under a sign reading: "You must be as tall as this sign to attack the city." The shortest Marine is taller than that sign, even if he has to crane his neck to look up at it.

Our sortie is to be a 2-v-1, with our Reserve lieutenant wingie ("Slinger") getting his first hours and fighting experience in the Hornet, our adversary on this occasion a TA-4 Mongoose in bizarre camouflage (to be flown by "Banger") from a visiting Navy Aggressor squadron. There will be four engagements in the planned forty-five-minute hop.

Since VFA-106 has a permanent DET at Fallon, a substantial proportion of the squadron's Hornets are on the line, both single- and two-seat versions, providing RAG/FRS squadron pilots—mostly from the East Coast F-4B/N and A-7E communities—with the opportunity to learn all about this spectacular airplane. We brief, suit up, check the records with maintenance control, and walk down in approved manner, and now have the chance to see this amazing new airplane up close, from behind the stick.

After the walkaround, with no problems identified, we climb in and strap it on, and Clam recites his preflight checklist on the internal communications system, energizes the internal auxiliary power unit to start the two GE engines, and checks wingie and adversary readiness before calling for and getting clearance from the Fallon tower. We taxi and launch in section, Slinger in tight, and it's time to look around the "office."

Information overload. That's the pilot's first impression of a Hornet "glass" cockpit with its three big multifunction displays, the HUD up on the glare shield. Everything is available instantly at the fingertips. HOTAS makes it much easier to fly and fight than its predecessor F-4s and A-7s.

What is it, then? What you have here, folks, is your Basic New-Age Fighter Plane, equipped with all the whistles and bells the taxpayers' money can buy (at $18 million per plane), performance to match.

Our Hornets separate from the A-4, which heads south, and fly north to the Dixie Valley, climbing to 25,000 feet effortlessly and seemingly instantaneously. As we reach the MOA's northern limits, we reverse to confront our A-4 adversary. The powerful Hughes radar picks him up more than thirty miles out, at our altitude, and as we close we tense for the fight.

One should be flying ACM daily to comprehend what is going on in these knife fights. And one should be fully conditioned to pulling G daily, with abandon, not just from time to time as an observer or participant. Part-time fighter pilots are literally out of it. The quickness of the hand on the stick deceives the eyeball trying to catch the action outside the window.

Not one of the encounters lasts longer than thirty seconds—thirty seconds that string out like hours as we try to outguess the A-4. From the backseat the view is impaired compared to that in the front, but it would be a lie to say that one could follow the fight without a program. Even a detailed prebrief on just what moves would be made would have been no help in this three-axis madness.

Four times we face the A-4, either as lead or wing. Four times we fight, from head on to astern. Four times the Hornet shows its devastating ability to turn, to pull Gs—G onset was never like this in the past, with 6, 7, and then more than 8G on the meter, the lungs and gut pressed firmly down on the asshole, the helmet forced down over the eyes, breath inhaled in brief bursts and held against the forces, greyout occurring despite all that grunting and tensing of neck muscles. Clam is nonchalant; at 5G+, in any attitude, he looks around with seeming ease, uses his left hand against the canopy to shield his eyes from the sun, peers back at our bogey, managing to swivel his head all the way round on one occasion ("to see back through the twin tails"), even swapping hands when he needs his right (stick) hand as a sun visor. Colonel Cool.

Three impressions stand out when reviewing the results: first, the Hornet's behavior at high angle of attack; second, G onset in the modern fighter; third, the extraordinary throttle authority of a bird with better than 1:1 thrust:weight when the fuel load gets low.

And turn!!! At high angle of attack, where the F-4 starts to rumble, shake, rock its wings at 16–17 units angle of attack, warning of imminent departure and the joys of a potential inverted flat spin, the Hornet is rock steady. Pull some more, you just get a buzz, a vibration, although at 35 units tortured vapor in the air condenses and pours back over the cockpit from the strakes, almost obscuring the rear closet.

G onset? You get it right now, and the GLOC (G-induced loss-of-consciousness) problem is real, even for pilots who are flying daily ACM hops. Flight physiology briefs GLOC, including a video that remains imprinted on the memory for life. And for Life.

Throttle authority is perhaps the most shatter-

ing. At 100 knots, throttle at idle, nose high, you can apply the burners and pull the nose up, then just accelerate upward in the vertical. Few other aircraft on the planet can stay with this sort of awesome power. The F-14D will be able to when it is reengined. These devices are becoming anti-gravity machines!

Back on the ground, Clam twinkles. "Nice hop," he says. "Like the Hornet?"

The correct answer: down to Strike's home-from-home in town, the Double Eagle Bar. At the Double Eagle, anything goes, and the ROE impose no rules at all except a willingness to push the envelope as hard and as long as the spirit moves and the spirits move. Balm for the body and mind, no TACTS to spy and pry, just the great camaraderie for which military aviation is justly famed, and the most fitting way to celebrate Strike ("Don't call it Strike U.")—with the Sierra Hotel Gang.

"Steely" Dan shows his radical technique for checking six.

Glossary:

Some of these terms, although used daily in the Fleet and at NSWC, may be unfamiliar to readers; some are offered tongue in cheek but are equally useful.

A/A, A/G Air-to-air, air-to-ground (also "air-to-mud")

AAA Antiaircraft artillery (usually called "triple A")

AAM Air-to-air missile (see also AIM)

AAR Air-to-air refueling ("gas")

ACLS Automatic Carrier Landing System electronic landing aid

ACM Air-combat maneuvering (dogfighting)—described by participants, e.g., 1-v-1 is one against one, 1-v-2 is one against two . . . 2-v-2, 1-v-many, 2-v-many, etc.

AEW Airborne early warning (E-2C Hawkeye, E-3 AWACS)

AGL Above ground level (altitude number)

AIM Air-intercept missile (e.g., AIM-7 Sparrow, AIM-9 Sidewinder, etc.)

ALCM Air-launched cruise missile

AOA Angle of attack, or alpha—degree to which aircraft is flown above unloaded or "zero alpha" condition (see also "G")—maximum "units" vary by aircraft type

ARM Antiradiation missile

ASW Antisubmarine warfare (P-3, S-3, SH-3 primarily)

Ball Also "meatball," Fresnel system lens used to guide pilot in routine carrier arrivals (see Traps)

Bandit Unknown A/A contact

BARCAP Barrier combat air patrol (see also CAP)

BIT Built-in test (on-board electronic system diagnosis)

B/N Bombardier/Navigator (A-6)

Bogey Confirmed bad-guy A/A contact

CAG Commander, air group (skipper of air wing)

CAP Combat air patrol (e.g., Hi-CAP, Lo-CAP, BARCAP)

Cat Steam catapult used to launch aircraft from carriers

CAVU Ceiling and visibility unlimited

CBU Cluster bomb unit

CEP Circular error probable (bomb-strike accuracy)

China Lake U.S. Naval Weapons Center, China Lake, California, longtime center for Navy A/A, A/G weapons development

CIC Combat information center (on carrier)

CNX Cancel

CSAR Combat search and rescue (see SAR)

C^3I Command, control, communications, intelligence (also older term C^2, or command and control)

CVW Carrier air wing

DACT Dissimilar air-combat training (see ACM)

Desert Mafia NSWC, MAWTS-1 (MCAS Yuma), VX-4 (NAS Pt. Mugu), VX-5 (China Lake), so called due to location/connectivity in strike-warfare development

DET: Detachment

E&E Evasion and escape after being "smoked" (shot down)

ECCM Electronic counter-countermeasures (anti-jamming)

ECM Electronic countermeasures (jamming)

ECMO Electronic countermeasures officer (EA-6B)

ELINT Electronic intelligence from various sources

Envelope Performance/operating limits of aircraft or missile

EO Electro-optical (lasers, infrared systems, etc.)

ESM Electronic support measures (passive EW sensors)

EW Electronic warfare (generic), also early warning

FAC Forward air controller (may be airborne or on ground)

FAST Fleet Air-Superiority Training

Feet dry Over the beach to the target, e.g., from the carrier

Feet wet Over the beach returning from target to carrier

FFARP Fleet Fighter ACM Readiness Program

FIST Fleet Integrated Suppression Training

FLIR Forward-looking infrared (target-detection system)

G Gravity, force of—when an aircraft is ''pulled'' by pulling back on the stick; high G/AOA/alpha is result

GCI Ground-controlled intercept (typically Soviet)

Gouge Informal inside information or scoop

HARM High-speed antiradiation missile

Harpoon Air-to-surface missile (A-6, A-7, F/A-18)

HAWK Home All the Way Killer (U.S. SAM system, sold by Lt. Col. Oliver North to Iran; also used worldwide by allies)

HOTAS Hands-on throttle and stick—technology that puts key flying/fighting/comm switches on throttle/stick, so pilot need not manipulate other cockpit switches while fighting, used in conjunction with HUD

HUD Head-up display, clear screen in front of pilot on the instrument-panel glare shield with fly/fight displays associated with HOTAS

IADS Integrated Air-Defense System, consisting of AAA and SAMs under radar guidance and central C^3I control

IFF Information Friend or Foe (aircraft electronic system)

IOC Initial operational capability after development and deployment

IR Infrared (used in missile seekers, for example, and for target imaging)

JTIDS Joint Tactical Information Display System (Air Force/Navy/Marine cockpit communications/display concept)

KISS Keep It Simple, Stupid

LAWES Light Attack Weapons Employment School (A-7 Top Gun)

Lemoore NAS Lemoore, West Coast Strike Community location

LGB Laser-guided bomb

LSO Landing-signal officer (guides recoveries on boat)

MAWES Medium Attack Weapons Employment School (A-6 Top Gun)

MAWTS-1 Marine Air Warfare Training Squadron One (Yuma, Arizona)

MER Multiple ejection rack (also see TER) for ordnance

MFD Multifunction display, TV-like screen in cockpit on which aircrew can command and view flying/fighting data

Miramar NAS Miramar, San Diego (''Fightertown, USA,'' and also famed location of Top Gun ACM training activity)

Moffett NAS Moffett Field, forty miles south of San Francisco, and West Coast P-3 ASW HQ (was Strike community HQ)

Mugu NAS Pt. Mugu, California (sixty miles north of Los Angeles)

NATOPS Naval Air Training and Operations program, used as basis for training manuals and daily aircrew testing

Nellis Nellis AFB, Air Force TAC (Tactical Air Command) HQ and location of USAF Red Flag training activity

North Island NAS North Island, San Diego, West Coast S-3/SH-3 ASW HQ on beach across town from NAS Miramar

NFO Naval flying officer (non-pilot air crew)

NSWC Naval Strike Warfare Center (at NAS Fallon, Nevada)

OAST Overland Air Superiority Training at NSWC/Top Gun

P^5 Prior Planning Prevents Poor Performance

PGM Precision-guided munitions

PK Probability of kill

Pop point Location for pull up into target-delivery maneuver from position close to ground; also verb "to pop"

—— **puke** *Attack* puke, *fighter* puke, etc., used in friendly conversation when referring to "other" community

ROE Rules of engagement, applying to all war or peacetime engagements and varied as appropriate to mission(s)

SAM Surface-to-air missile

SAR Search and rescue

SEAD (pronounced "see-add") Suppression of enemy air defenses

SFWE Strike Fighter Weapons Employment (F/A-18 A/G Top Gun; see LAWES, MAWES)

SHRIKE Type of ARM

SLATS Strike Leader Attack Training Syllabus (strike lead academics) at NSWC

TACTS Tactical Air Combat Training System— pods carried on aircraft missile stations that relay aircraft behavior to ground receivers for computer storage/display/review

TAD Temporarily assigned duty (compare USAF "TDY")

TAMPS Tactical Aircraft Mission Planning System (computer)

TARPS Tactical Air Reconnaissance Pod System (for F-14), usually used for pre- and post-strike target review

TEAMS Tactical Electronic (Warfare) Aircraft Missile Support (computer)

TER Triple ejection rack (see also MER) for ordnance

Terrain masking Use of terrain (hills, mountains) to prevent one's aircraft from being observed by enemy radar

Tomahawk Surface-to-surface cruise missile

TOT Time over target

Traps Recovery of aircraft on carrier via trapping on deck through aircraft hook engagement of deck wires

VID Visual identification (typically of ACM adversary)

Viz Visibility (weather related)

Whidbey NAS Whidbey Island, WA, West Coast A-6/EA-6B HQ

WX Weather report or briefing

Danny Ferrington

About the Author

John Joss is an aviation writer who has written extensively for major media worldwide about air warfare and associated computer and electronic technologies. He is a current, active pilot, and has flown, or flown in, most of the fighter and attack aircraft in the current U.S. inventory.

About the Photographer

George Hall is one of the world's premier photographers of military aviation. His work has appeared in scores of books including TOP GUN (which he also wrote), USAFE, RED FLAG, MARINE AIR, CV: CARRIER AVIATION, and also in the annual AIRPOWER calendar.